SECURITY & SAFETY
IN THE HOME

HAMLYN PRACTICAL DIY GUIDES HOMEBASE

SECURITY & SAFETY IN THE HOME

John McGowan & Roger DuBern

HAMLYN

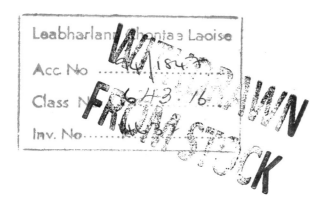
ACKNOWLEDGMENTS

Copy editor:
John Stace

•

Technical consultant
Mike Trier

•

Art editors:
Lee Griffiths and Bob Gordon

•

Design:
Crucial Books

•

Special photography:
Jon Bouchier

•

Illustration:
Oxford Illustrators Limited
Ron Hayward
Patrick Mulrey

•

Picture research:
Emily Hedges

•

Production controller:
Helen Seccombe

This edition published in 1990 by
The Hamlyn Publishing Group Limited
a division of
The Octopus Publishing Group
Michelin House
81 Fulham Road
LONDON SW3 6RB

© The Hamlyn Publishing Group
Limited 1990

ISBN 0-600-565 88-2

Printed in Belgium by PROOST N.V.

**The publishers thank the following
organisations for their kind permission
to reproduce the following pictures in
this book:**
Telecom Security 45
Elizabeth Whiting & Associates 3
Rentokil 94
John Walmsley 8, 9
Zefa 6

**The publishers thank the following
manufacturers who supplied products
for photography:**
Black & Decker; Chubb Lock Company;
First Alert; Polycell Products; Siesta
Leisure; Vitrex; Yale Security Products.

All other subjects for special
photography supplied by Sainsbury's
Homebase.

CONTENTS

INTRODUCTION

Two aspects of home improvements that are likely to be overlooked completely are security and safety. Yet they are vital ingredients in any modern home.

Arguably, security and safety could be the basis on which any house is replanned. Strangely, as far as the former is concerned, few estate agents up to now have included security as part of the sales blurb when trying to sell a house. Yet, if we were to read that "all doors and windows are fitted with high-security locks" or "the home is protected by a complete burglar alarm system" we would see these as being great advantages.

The same is true of safety. Why is the emphasis not placed more on the fact that safety glass is fitted in all doors? What about the fact that the consumer unit is fitted with miniature circuit breakers instead of ordinary fuses?

Yet we as home owners with families know the importance of security and safety – and in the following pages you can discover how to bring your home right up to scratch.

SECURITY

Nowadays we are all very well aware that crime is on the increase – in particular certain crimes such as house burglary. It is an extremely nasty crime since it is a violation of our privacy and our home by total strangers. It is an experience that can cause severe nervous illness to those unfortunate enough to become a victim. In some cases, people have had to move from a house they have been in for many years, a home they loved, because of the traumatic effect that a burglary has had on them. *They no longer feel at ease in their own home.*

If you are sensible you will make sure that your home contents are well covered by insurance. However, although that may mean that you will have a new video recorder or television set to replace the one that has been stolen, no amount of money can ever replace more treasured, personal items. In this section of the book, you can find out what measures you can take to protect your home from thieves.

GENERAL ADVICE

Many people still harbour a romantic picture of a burglar — a nocturnal creature entering and searching a house in an almost orderly manner and taking some valuables and money before leaving as silently as he came, his visit discovered only when the family get up in the morning.

If you are lucky your burglar might fit this picture. Assuming everyone in the house is able to cope with the traumatic shock and your insurance will cover the cost of stolen items, then you will have got off lightly.

The other side of the coin can be devastating.

Imagine returning tired but happy from an evening out or a holiday and finding your home wrecked. It is not uncommon for people to be confronted with this situation. Imagine seeing furniture smashed, broken glass strewn around, liquids poured over carpets, curtains and upholstery, clothes cupboards turned out and the contents ripped apart. Peculiarly, the intruders might not even have stolen anything — such savage, wanton vandalism can be carried out by thugs just for kicks.

It is essential, therefore, that you ensure your home should be as secure as possible.

Such a sight might greet you after your home has been ransacked.

It is a sad fact of life that nowadays we must all be more security conscious. Each one of us is a potential burglary victim – it is no longer the rich who have most to fear, as soaring burglary statistics prove.

Ask yourself if your house is secure – or if it is a soft touch for intruders. Do you have careless habits like leaving doors open or unlocked while you pop out for ten minutes? If so, watch out: tomorrow it could be your turn to suffer.

By far the greatest number of burglaries occur in the afternoon and early evening, between 3 p.m. and 8 p.m. Well over half are carried out by children and youths. Basically these are sneak thieves who take advantage of open windows and doors and will enter and leave in seconds, snatching money or anything portable that has been left lying around. Sometimes they do not even have to come inside a house: items left on the inside sill of an open window are easily taken.

Do not be tricked

Burglars and sneak thieves use all sorts of tricks to get into houses. Sometimes they work in pairs, with one keeping a housewife chatting at the front door while an accomplice gets in through a back door.

Phone calls purporting to be from school saying little Billy has been taken ill and 'can you come quickly' are a method of enticing mum from the house, leaving it empty for the thief (who made the call and has watched her leave) to help himself.

In a similar vein is the call from the 'local police' received shortly after keys are lost. You are invited around to the station immediately and while you are gone the burglar lets himself in your front door. He made the call, of course!

If you ever get such a call, check the number of the school, police station or whatever yourself in the directory (do not accept the number the caller may give you) then ring back to authenticate the call.

Losing keys creates a dilemma – especially when they are on a ring or in a purse containing your address. Even if you receive your keys back from the police quickly or in the post from a seemingly decent finder, there is always the chance that they may have been copied.

The only safe thing to do is to have the lock tumblers, levers and barrels changed – which is less expensive than changing the complete lock. And remember, never carry keys on a ring or in a purse or bag that can lead the finder to your home.

Finally, on the subject of keys, do not leave them on a piece of string behind the letterbox or under the doormat. Burglars are only too aware of these tricks – no hiding place, however clever you may think it, is likely to remain undiscovered by a determined and experienced professional.

Check the identity of all callers.

Of course, there is the crude, dangerous intruder who will force himself into a house when the door is opened – particularly vulnerable here are the elderly or persons living alone. Anyone in this situation should check the identity of callers from a side window overlooking the front door, or by fitting a peephole viewer in the door. A strong guard chain is essential. Telephone-style intercom systems are another asset in certain cases.

The con man, pretending to be from the council, gas board, or whatever, is another common threat. Any unexpected calls from such 'officials' can be dealt with by asking them to wait outside while you phone their office – again look up the number for yourself or ask the operator. And remember, gas boards and so on will make personalised arrangements for blind people who have to be visited – if you have any blind friends or relatives make sure they know about these arrangements.

Do not accept any identity cards, however authentic they appear, as absolute proof of identification. If in any doubt, make a phone call to check the identity.

Good neighbours

The police stress that if we were all better neighbours and more observant we would be helping each other and helping them to combat burglary. If any suspicious persons or strangers are seen hanging around they should be reported immediately.

There are many other things we can do. For example, never discuss holiday plans loudly in public – you never know who may be listening. Delivery people such as the milkman should be told verbally about periods away – never leave notes.

A trustworthy neighbour can be of great help during holidays by mak-

Avoid tell-tale signs of absence

ing sure that post, newspapers and so on are not left protruding from the letterbox. A neighbour can also help give the house an occupied look by popping in during the evenings to switch on the lights for a couple of hours. Or you can fit one of the automatic devices which switch lights on and off at preset times. Drawing the curtains also helps, as does keeping the lawn cut during a long absence.

If you are just going out for an evening, a bedroom and living room light left on is a good idea – so, too, is leaving a transistor radio on.

A house with all the windows shut on a summer's day is a telltale sign that it is empty. This creates a dilemma. If you are just off to the coast for the day, you would not feel too happy about leaving windows open. The sensible compromise would be to leave an inaccessible window open and locked in that position with a suitable security device.

A similar dilemma arises when deciding whether or not to lock internal doors. Once a thief is inside a house, he is free to use whatever force he likes to open a door. On the other hand, the thief might not like making any kind of noise and so might be deterred. On balance, it is probably best to lock doors at night when the house is occupied but leave them open when you are out. At night, a locked door will often confine a burglar to the room he has entered through a window.

On any security measure when there is a dilemma, or special circumstances, or where advice of a general nature is needed, it is worth while asking at the police station to be put in touch with the local crime prevention officer.

The local CPO can also tell you how to go about setting up a Neighbourhood Watch scheme in your road if one does not already exist.

Commonsense

Remember that most of us can avoid becoming a burglary victim by commonsense measures. Burglars never want to hang around outside a house for very long – for obvious reasons. When a burglar is hunting for a house to enter, he will overlook any which present a problem in the sure knowledge that he will find easier meat elsewhere. So your first step should be always to lock windows and doors at night or in the daytime when they are not being guarded by someone's presence in the vicinity.

VULNERABLE POINTS

Every house has its weak points. Burglars can spot them immediately and such weaknesses determine which houses they favour — those that they can enter quickly and quietly without being seen or making any noise. Here and overleaf, we highlight some of the suspect places at the front and back of the house. This will help you identify vulnerable parts of your own property. So stand back and take a long look all round — imagine you are a burglar 'casing' a house for an easy way in.

If you arrived home and discovered that you had lost your keys, what would you do — presuming no-one else who has keys is contactable? This simple exercise can be both informative and alarming — in no time you will have identified the weak points in your house security system.

What is it likely to be in your case? Is the side gate always left unlocked, allowing you to walk around to the back of the house where you know the open kitchen window or patio doors will let you get inside? Or is the garage door always unlocked as well as the internal door giving access from the garage to the house?

Is the sliding window over the porch always unlocked ready to be pushed back? All you need is a ladder to get you on to the porch roof — and that is kept in the back garden by the fence. It is all too easy. Far too many people will find this a familiar story.

Anyone who concludes that there is no way in without breaking a window can be happy with their defences. Or can they? Well, at least your burglar will be delayed for a while and will then have to make a noise to gain entry. Yet it is a far from perfect situation. Not all burglars put a brick through a window — some use a glass cutter to take out a pane of glass quietly. In any case, if you can break glass in order to get through, or to reach through to open a door or the window itself, then you are still very vulnerable. You really need to think of fitting toughened glass and locks and handles which cannot be operated even if they can be reached from outside.

Fences and gates

Take a look at your first line of defence. Many houses, of course, do not have a fence or hedge surrounding the front garden, so your burglar can approach the front door easily. However, you may well have a side gate, which is the first obstacle he will encounter. The first thing is that, irrespective of its material, the gate should be locked. It is true that a six-foot high gate can be climbed easily — but few burglars would want to risk attracting that sort of attention. In any case, a locked gate

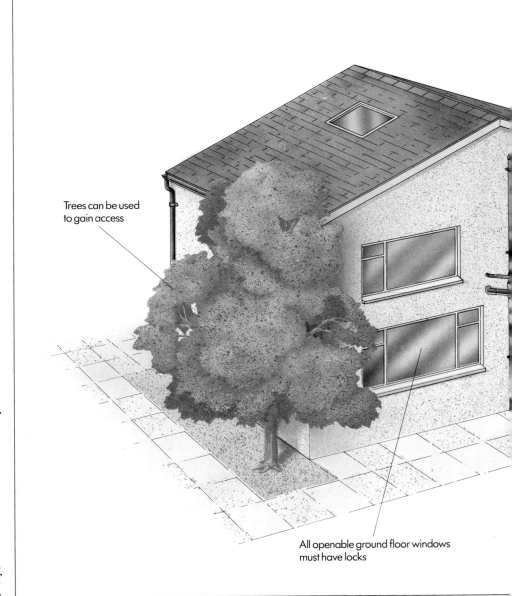

Trees can be used to gain access

All openable ground floor windows must have locks

may also prevent items, certainly heavy or bulky things, from being carried away down a side alley. Admittedly the lock on a side gate may be simple to force – but that means making a noise, which most burglars are reluctant to do.

Many people imagine that a property with a field at the back is especially vulnerable since the rear of the house is immediately accessible to the burglar. However, this is not necessarily the case since he can be easily spotted approaching and leaving the house. This in one sense can make a house with an open rear aspect a less desirable target. There are plenty of houses with sheltered areas at the back which are a better bet for a burglar.

High fences and walls, though not offering a real barrier to the burglar, since they can be climbed, do create a psychological barrier. A wall can be made a more difficult obstacle by making the top course of bricks cas-tellated or pointed to make it difficult to create a handhold.

A thick hawthorn bush is a real challenge but is not something that you can just put there – it takes years for it to grow.

Next have a look around the house and study any trees close to the building. Could an agile burglar use the tree or thick ivy as a ladder to give direct access to a window or to the roof of an extension or garage which would then bring a window within reach? If so, then presuming you do not want to get rid of an established tree, you will have to make that window really secure.

Never make the mistake of thinking that a small window, in a toilet for example, is safe because a burglar could not squeeze through it. Burglars come in all shapes and sizes and sometimes they are accompanied by a child who is lifted through a small window and is then able to open up a door or large window for the others to get in.

Skylight roofs would seem to be completely safe purely because of their position. Not so: a sloping roof is as good as a roof ladder to a burglar with a head for heights.

Drainpipes

Regard any window or roof which can be reached from a drainpipe as a real weak link. Drainpipes should be thought of as ladders ready for use.

You cannot remove drainpipes but you can make them more difficult to climb by coating them with an anti-climb paint. This does two things: it makes the pipe greasy and leaves a sticky deposit on the climber's hands. The thing to remember is that you should not coat the bottom six or seven feet of pipe in case family or visitors lean against it.

Natural ladders are one thing. To leave a real ladder lying around is enormously careless – in many cases you might as well leave the front door open. Your ladder must be kept under lock and key – and out of sight – in a garage or shed. If you have to store it outside then lock it to a fence or wall with a padlock on it.

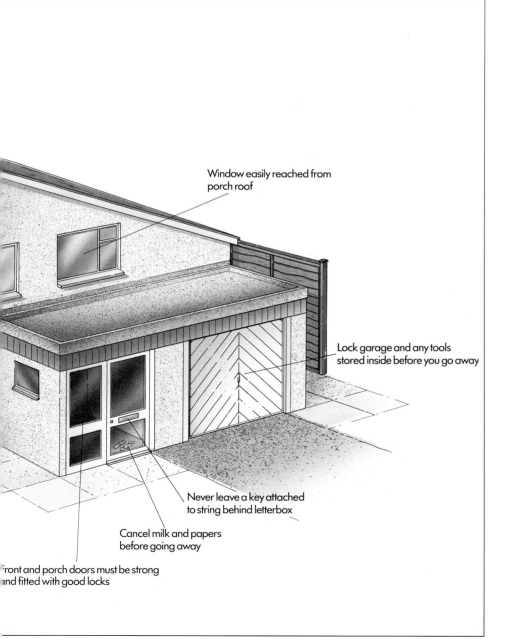

Window easily reached from porch roof

Lock garage and any tools stored inside before you go away

Never leave a key attached to string behind letterbox

Cancel milk and papers before going away

Front and porch doors must be strong and fitted with good locks

Front door

The front door of a house is the classic entry point for a burglar. If he can open this quickly, then he has also got a large exit through which he can carry bulky items such as a video or portable television.

It is not often appreciated that in a classic suburban road in mid-morning or afternoon groups of houses on both sides of the street can be completely empty, with the occupants at work, school, on holiday or shopping trips. Very often the 'front' or main door may not even face the road – it might be tucked out of sight around the side of the house, giving a burglar a perfect concealed spot in which to work.

A favourite ploy of a burglar is to knock at a door to see if anyone is in. This is the quickest way to establish with reasonable certainty that the house is empty. If someone opens the door then he can pretend to be a salesman or someone who has arrived at the wrong address.

The next stage is to get through the door. It is quite amazing how many front doors still have the original, simple cylinder latch fitted as the only means of protection.

This is the type of lock that is replaced or augmented when the damage is done and the burglar has been inside. It is a very easy lock for a professional thief to get past. He might have to break a small adjacent window to be able to reach through and open up but this type of lock can usually be forced with just a piece of celluloid.

A door fitted with just a simple cylinder lock is an inviting target – it should have a mortise lock as well. The presence of such a lock tells the burglar that even if he breaks a small window he will not be able to open the door since the occupants will have locked it from the outside.

A glazed door – fully or partly glazed – obviously presents a greater weakness compared with a solid oak door. A fully glazed door is probably safer than one split into two or more panels simply because it makes a louder noise if broken.

However, if a burglar is prepared to smash down a glass door, it is probably because the house is fairly isolated or he is prepared to burst in and out in seconds taking with him cash or small portable objects.

The best answer here is either to fit a wrought-iron grille behind the glass or to use wired or toughened glass. Toughened glass will resist a sledge hammer, so although a burglar might try to smash it down he is unlikely to succeed. A wrought-iron grille is obviously off-putting and it need not be grim-looking – there are plenty of attractive ornamental grilles around, some being supplied in kit form for assembly and fixing to a door or window.

An extra line of defence is provided by a porch – no burglar wants to have to get through two doors in order to break into a house. So provided that your porch door is fitted with a good quality mortise lock – and it is kept locked at relevant

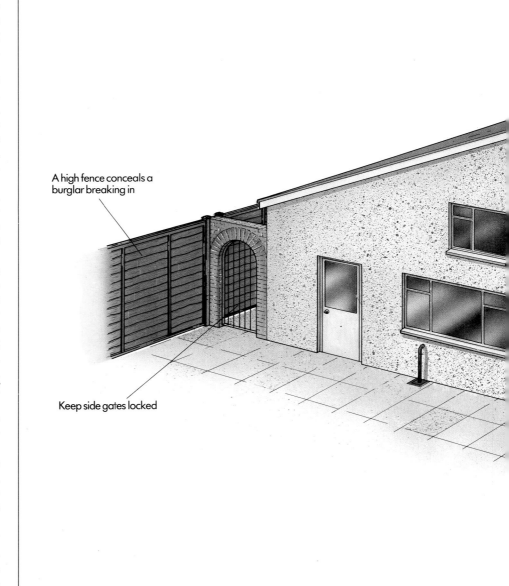

A high fence conceals a burglar breaking in

Keep side gates locked

times – you have double protection.

Obviously the design of a porch is important from the security viewpoint, as much as anything else. A porch that virtually conceals the front door is an ideal position from which a thief can work his way quietly into the house. A fully glazed porch, however, hides nothing.

That, though, has a built-in disadvantage. Letters, circulars, and free newspapers pushed through the letterbox may be left to lie on the floor – possibly for days on end at holiday times. If your porch allows a burglar to see inside you should fit a box into which deliveries will fall.

Understandably, many people value their privacy and plant hedges of conifers and suchlike to screen windows and doors from passers-by. This has one obvious drawback – it also provides a screen for a burglar trying to break in. So it is a question of deciding whether your privacy or security is more important to you.

Lighting

Privacy is one of a burglar's best friends. Darkness is another. You can deter him easily on the second count by making sure the front of the house is well illuminated after dark. The basic idea is to illuminate any secluded area, starting at the front gate and working towards the house. There are various types of light available and it is the type, number and location of each that is important. Obviously, you need to light the front door and porch area, vulnerable downstairs windows and any upstairs windows which are accessible. Lighting, as you can read in detail later, can be operated manually, by sensor switches or by time controls.

The other major concern on ground-floor level is the windows. You should regard all these as being a great risk, with windows that open being particularly dangerous. Among the most vulnerable types are louvred windows, patio doors and leaded lights.

All opening windows, however, should have excellent locks fitted. The best possible security is provided by double glazing.

Too many people concentrate on securing the house and completely forget about the garage. A garage will have a front entrance and, possibly, a single door elsewhere or a window. If the garage is attached to the house it may well have a connecting door.

The problem with a garage is that it tends to house an arsenal of equipment which, ironically, a burglar can borrow to break into your home – apart from the possibility of valuable tools and equipment themselves being stolen along with any other items being stored. So do treat your garage as part of the house and make sure the burglar stays outside.

In the same vein, pay a lot of attention to the garden shed. Here he can also find the right equipment with which to break in. Garden sheds are often at the end of the garden so making a noise to get inside them is less of a risk.

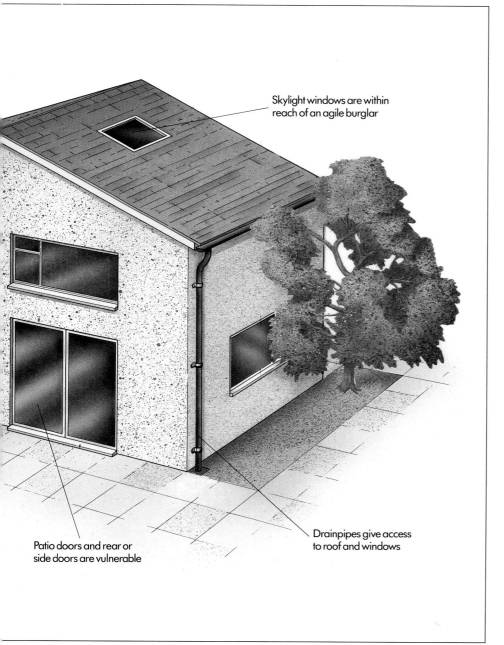

Skylight windows are within reach of an agile burglar

Drainpipes give access to roof and windows

Patio doors and rear or side doors are vulnerable

DEVICES, ALARMS AND LOCKS

The past few years have seen huge advances in the types and quality of locks and alarms that are readily available to help home owners secure their property. Long gone are the days when a simple barrel bolt or a flimsy chain would suffice.

When break-ins started to become so frequent, there was an immediate demand for more substantial defences. Then, as burglars became more sophisticated and knowledgeable in ways of overcoming the new family of locks and alarms, manufacturers responded by producing even better systems. At last, the battle is being won — at least in those houses where the owners have recognised that statistically they are likely to become a victim unless they protect themselves.

It cannot be overemphasized that anything you can do to prolong the time it takes, or to increase the amount of noise that is necessary for an intruder to make to get into your house, will substantially reduce the chances of your being burgled.

On the next few pages a bewildering array of security devices and alarms is displayed. The immediate reaction can be to imagine that the whole business of security is far too complex for the average person to grasp and use to their advantage.

Do not be too hasty. What we are demonstrating to you is that there is such an assortment of products available that you will be able to provide yourself with a sophisticated, tailor-made security system to protect your home and family.

Even though it is tailor-made, it is available to you instantly, off-the-shelf. Once you know what you need, you can make a shopping list and then spend an enjoyable weekend fitting your locks and bolts and, by the end of it, you will have the enormous satisfaction of a job well done and a tremendous increase in peace of mind — something that, these days, no one can put a price on.

First, then, do not be 'alarmed'. You do not need all the items dis-

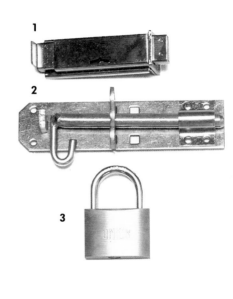

1 Shed lock;
2 Padbolt;
3 Open-shackle
padlock; *4* 7-day
plug-in timeswitch;
5 Personal attack
alarm; *6* Code-
operated door
alarm; *7* Security
scriber and
invisible marker;
8 Passive infrared
sensor and sensor
switch; *9* Floor
safe; *10* PIR globe
wall lantern;
11 Low-voltage
garden spotlight;
12 Smoke alarm
with emergency
light; *13* Fire
extinguisher

10   11   12   13

played here – if you did then you would be turning your home into a virtual Fort Knox! This would mean that you must have some extreme valuables on the premises – and, if so, your enemy would not be the run-of-the-mill burglar but a highly sophisticated, determined professional who might well be prepared to spend the time and effort necessary to get in despite any barriers you put

up. You would really then be moving into a whole new ball game.

A normal home needs only a handful of these items to have maximum protection. It does not matter what type of windows or doors your home has – whether they are hinged or sliding; timber, steel or plastic; new or old – you can find a security device to protect them.

The people most frightened by this display are would-be intruders. The number of houses which are 'easy pickings' is growing less and less each month. Whereas in the past a road of houses was an 'open invitation', nowadays, the intruder has to try quite a few addresses before he is 'allowed in'.

The purpose of this book is to help you to identify, buy and fit the best devices for your situation so that you get best value-for-money protection. Nothing is more disappointing than

to find you have spent a lot of money on something that will not do the job you expected of it. So never buy anything until you are completely satisfied that it is exactly what you need for your specific purpose.

There are plenty of things to watch for – such as the type of door or window, thickness of material, position of surrounding framework and so on. You also need to make sure that excellent detailed instructions are provided so that you can get on and fit the device without hitches. Do not waste your time and money on any product that fails to meet these requirements. There are plenty of manufacturers who are sufficiently proud of their products and who are sufficiently interested in their customers to ensure that success and performance of their products are guaranteed.

Throughout this book you will find guidance on locks and bolts for every situation. You will easily be able to sort out what you need and to see how each device is fitted as we take you through the stages. Some are more complicated to fit than others, though this does not necessarily mean that they will give better security or protection.

One thing it will highlight is whether or not you have sufficient DIY skills in order to install any

particular device. The vast majority of devices require only basic skills and a few normal household tools – drill, screwdriver and so on. Others are a little more tricky and though the average handyperson will have no problems, it is understandable that many people may prefer to call in a tradesman to do the actual fitting.

In this case you will find this book invaluable in helping you to select the ideal fittings for your specific purpose. You will then be able to buy all you need and hand your 'shopping basket' to your tradesman or give him a detailed list.

Although all the information you need to help you choose your devices is to be found on the following pages, if you have any doubts at all do not be afraid to get on-the-spot expert advice. Your local crime prevention officer will be only too pleased to visit your home to chat over things personally. Get in touch with your C.P.O. through the police station.

To provide whole-house protection does not necessarily involve a huge financial outlay – even if you are virtually starting from scratch because your home, at present, has only basic locks on the front and

back door. Of course, the larger the house and the greater the number of vulnerable windows, the deeper you will have to dig into your pocket: but the average 'two-down, three-up semi' will have only two exterior doors and perhaps no more than a dozen vulnerable windows to protect as a basic measure – in this case you are not likely to be breaking the bank to get what you need.

If you are restricted to a very limited budget then invest, initially, on protection for the doors and most vulnerable windows. You can gradually add to your system of defences month by month as quickly as possible.

It is not possible to be more specific than that here when generalising. Houses come in so many shapes

and sizes and with so many window and door arrangements that you need to decide on your own order of priorities – or perhaps get on-the-spot advice from your local C.P.O.

Finally, in the same way that some people buy things such as exercise bikes but soon 'forget' to use them, some people buy expensive locks and bolts and then, having showed them off to the neighbours, rarely bother to engage them. Find a way of making it a habit always to use your security system when it is needed.

Insurance

One of the advantages of fitting good security is that your insurance policy can cost you less. Insurance companies are now offering inducements to policy holders who have taken the trouble to fit locks and alarms in their home.

It will certainly pay you to shop around since companies vary enor-mously in what they are prepared to offer. Normally you can expect certain percentages to be lopped off the basic cost of a premium for the type and amount of locks fitted. This can depend on circumstances such as the type of property, accessibility and location – some areas are considered to be a far greater risk than others.

You will certainly need to do your sums here since many insurance companies are adept in concealing what they really mean. An offer to reduce premiums by, say, 20 per cent for a property having locks and bolts fitted can be very appealing when taken at face value but it could be disguising the fact that the initial premium is far higher than any other company would offer: you could be no better off, perhaps even worse off in the end.

So go through the 'offers' carefully. What is meant by 'approved' locks for example? And by whom? And are they required to be fitted professionally to be accepted?

Of course, some companies take the opposite view and start you off at a normal premium and then add loadings to properties which do not have certain locks and bolts fitted.

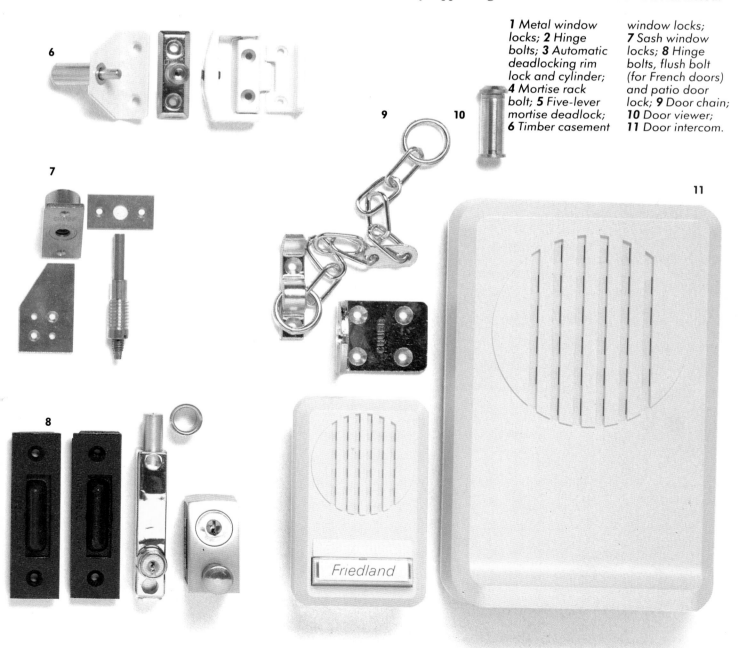

1 Metal window locks; 2 Hinge bolts; 3 Automatic deadlocking rim lock and cylinder; 4 Mortise rack bolt; 5 Five-lever mortise deadlock; 6 Timber casement window locks; 7 Sash window locks; 8 Hinge bolts, flush bolt (for French doors) and patio door lock; 9 Door chain; 10 Door viewer; 11 Door intercom.

DOORS

External doors have to fulfil two roles — they have to keep thieves out, and they must keep property in. Far too often they are fitted with only rudimentary locks, such as a nightlatch or non-deadlocking cylinder rim latch on the front door, and a two-lever mortise lock on the back door.

This means that if a burglar gains entry through a window, he has no difficulty in leaving, with your property, through the front or back door. Even when better quality locks are fitted, it is surprising how many people leave keys for burglars to find.

Another important factor is the type and strength of the door which is fitted. Do not buy an external door purely on its appearance, and remember that the more secluded the door, the stronger and more protected it should be.

There are various types of external doors. Flush doors, which have flat, smooth surfaces on each side may be made for external use, but generally they are too flimsy to give adequate security and they should be replaced with a panelled door.

Panelled doors are generally made from solid timber rails which are mortise-and-tenon jointed to form a substantial frame which may be filled with panels of solid timber, plywood, or glass. Ideally, the panels will be solid wood or plywood. If glass must be used to give light into the house, then make sure it is laminated or the toughened safety glass type. Leaded lights are particularly weak, and in a front door they should be reinforced behind with metal retaining bars.

Hardwood doors are generally, but not always, stronger than softwood types. A better guide to quality may be the thickness of an external door which should be a minimum of 44mm (1¾in).

In addition to a strong door, good locks are required. For a back door you need a good quality mortise lock and bolts top and bottom. For a front door, a cylinder rim latch or nightlatch will be required for convenience of opening and closing the door quickly. For security, the latch should be capable of being deadlocked which means that the bolt cannot be moved back unless the key is used. The door should have bolts at top and bottom for use at night, a door viewer so you can find out who is outside before opening the door, and a door chain to limit the extent to which the door can be opened and so prevent the forced entry of a barge-in thief.

Door viewer

Door chain

Hinge bolt

Mortise lock

Mortise rack bolt

Rim lock

Rim locks

There are basically two types of external door locks – rim locks and mortise locks.

Rim locks screw to the surface of a door and are easy to fit. They have a spring-operated latch with a rounded face which automatically springs back when the door is shut to hold the door closed. To open the door the latch can be turned back using a key or internal knob or moving a sliding handle.

Mortise locks fit into a mortise (a slot) in the edge of the door so they are very neat, and a good quality lock, correctly fitted, gives good security.

1 Position the paper template on inside of door. Mark centre hole for cylinder and screws with bradawl.

2 Make hole for lock cylinder using large bit or drill ring of smaller holes. Mark connecting bar for cutting.

3 Fit the lock backplate. Use a try square to make sure it is positioned level before fixing.

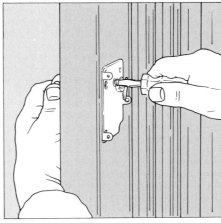

4 Insert the key in the cylinder to hold it steady, then secure it to the backplate.

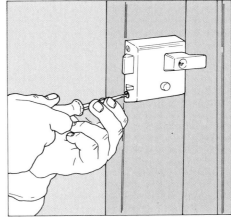

5 Fit the lock body by engaging the locating peg in the backplate hole and screw the lock case on.

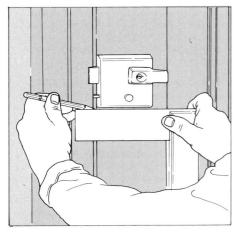

6 Close the door and use the lock body to mark the position of the staple plate.

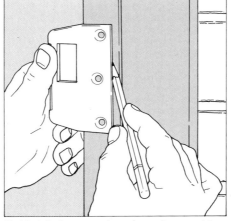

7 Hold the staple plate in position and mark around the edge. Carefully chisel out a recess for the plate.

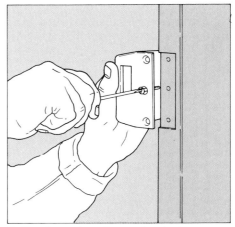

8 Replace the plate, check the operation of the lock. If all is well, screw the staple plate in position.

Because a rim lock is screwed to the surface of a door, it does not weaken it in the way that a mortise lock does. So it is much more suitable for a thinner door than a mortise lock – when a door is forced it is almost always the wood rather than the lock which gives way.

Also, the staple of a rim lock (the box into which the springbolt catches), does not weaken the frame on which it is surface mounted. But on the other hand, because it is held only by screws, it is difficult to mount securely.

Because the main fixing screws of both the rim lock and its staple are on the edge of the door, they are protected from removal when the door is closed, but it is possible that the lock will be prised bodily off the door, splitting the wood in the process.

There are various types of rim locks, the simplest being a nightlatch which functions as a spring-loaded latch to hold a door closed. The latch is operated by a key from the outside and by a knob from inside. In its most basic form this type offers virtually no security because it is so easily opened, either by turning the handle after breaking an adjacent sheet of glass, by pushing back the springbolt with a piece of flexible plastic, or by simply forcing the door open. In practice, even simple rim locks have a deadlocking mechanism operated by a snib from the inside which prevents the springbolt from being forced back, but this gives no security when the house is unoccupied.

For good security either an automatically deadlocking rim latch (automatic deadlock) or a deadlockable latch is required. The automatic deadlock has a springbolt with a mechanism that prevents the bolt from being forced back when the door is shut. It should also be possible to deadlock the internal handle by using a key from either the outside, or from the inside. When fitted within reach of a glass panel, deadlocking latches are essential, and they are useful in any case because

they prevent intruders from leaving easily.

When selecting a rim latch it is a good idea to look for one made to BS 3621. Remember that there is considerable variation in the sizes of locks and small-body latches are available to suit doors with narrow stiles.

Mortise locks

Because the body of a mortise lock is concealed within the thickness of a door no part of it is visible when the door is closed and therefore it is less likely to be tampered with or forced,

especially if it is made to BS 3621. Cutting the slot for the lock does weaken the door, so do not fit a lock of this type to a door less than 44mm (1¾in) thick, or, in the case of a glass panelled door, with stiles less than 63mm (2½in) wide. If you are worried about the strength of a door fitted with a mortise lock, door reinforcing kits are available. Neat reinforcing plates fit over the lock position on the surface of the door on each side, and an expanding bolt is driven into the striker box to reinforce the frame.

When choosing a mortise lock, re-

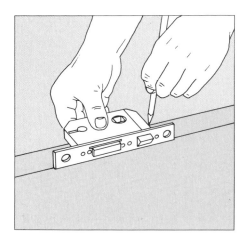

1 Hold the lock in position on the door edge (either before or after hanging) and mark the size of the mortise slot required on the door.

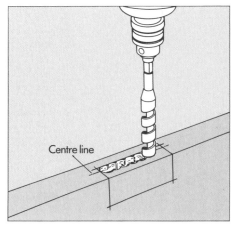

2 Mark a centre line on the edge of the door and roughly drill out the mortise slot to the depth of the lock case.

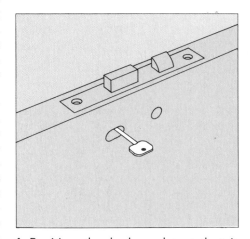

6 Position the lock and test that it operates smoothly. Screw it in place and add handles and escutcheon plates.

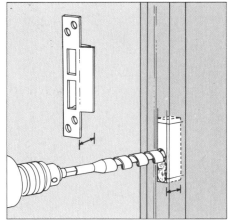

7 Operate the bolt, then close door to mark the bolt and latch positions on the frame. Drill the frame for the striking plate box.

member that lock cases are available in different widths to suit the width of the door stile. For glass panel doors choose a narrow-stile mortise lock.

There are basically two types of mortise locks – the key-operated deadbolt and the two-bolt mortise lock, or sash bolt. The latter has both a latchbolt and a deadbolt. The latchbolt is operated from either side by the door handle, and the deadbolt is operated by key. Generally, two-bolt mortise locks are fitted on back and side doors, while key-operated deadbolts are fitted to front doors to give additional security to that provided by a rim latch.

While rim locks are operated by cylinders containing pin tumblers, most mortise locks are operated by levers. The number of levers determines the security level of the lock. The more levers there are, the greater the number of key variations, and the securer the lock. A two-lever lock, for example, has very little security value, while a five-lever lock gives a high level of security. For very high security, some mortise locks are cylinder-operated, and it is possible to get two similar cylinders so that the same key can be used to operate both front and back doors.

Fitting a mortise lock in a replacement door requires a fair degree of skill, as the step-by-step sequence shows. However, when upgrading or replacing an existing lock it is often possible to fit a new mortise lock straight into an existing mortise slot with very little modification to the slot, handle or keyhole positions. When fitting or replacing more than one mortise lock, you can order them with "keys to pass" – one key will operate all the locks.

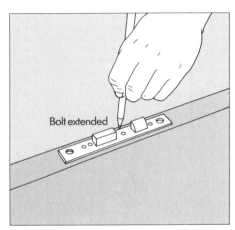

3 Smooth the sides of the mortise slot using a chisel, then position the lock (with the bolt extended) and mark around the faceplate.

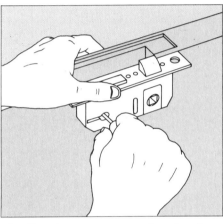

4 Chisel out a recess for the face-plate, then hold the lock against the door edge and mark the key and latch holes with a bradawl.

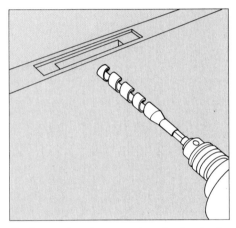

5 Bore the key and spindle holes through the door stile. Shape the key hole by drilling two overlapping smaller holes.

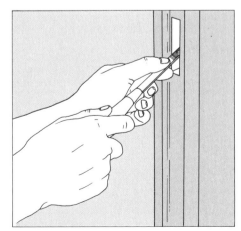

8 Chisel out a slot in the frame for the striking plate box, and keep trying it to ensure a snug fit – any looseness will reduce the security.

9 Mark round the faceplate of the box and chisel out a recess for the plate to lie flush with the surface of the rebate in the frame.

10 Finally, screw the striking plate in position using as large screws as possible, but ensure that the heads lie flush with the faceplate.

Mortise rack bolt

The mortise rack bolt is the best type of bolt for an external door. Fitted at the top and bottom of a door, it gives the door rigidity, and with the door securely fastened at three points (the centre is held by means of the rim latch and/or mortise locks) it is virtually impossible to force open.

A mortise rack bolt comprises a cylindrical bolt shoot encased in a barrel which is mortised into a hole drilled in the door edge. The bolt shoot has a row of teeth on one side which engage in the splines of a special removable key. Turning the key winds out the bolt which locks in position. By being set in the door edges, these bolts are difficult to tamper with, and because the bolt shoots a considerable distance into the door frame, they are virtually impossible to break out. The only problem with them is that they are all operated by a universal splined key, so the lockable bolt is gaining in popularity. In this case the bolt shoot is locked with a key to prevent it from being withdrawn. Some types are self-locking and the key is used only to unlock them.

Hinge bolt

Hinges are really vulnerable on doors that open outwards because the hinge pins are exposed and it is easy for an intruder to drive out the pins and prise open the door from the hinge side. Occasionally, even a conventional door is forced open on the hinge side.

These occurrences can be prevented by fitting hinge bolts. These are studs set into the hinge edge of a door which engage into sockets on the frame. The hinge bolts are fitted close to the door hinges; two or three are sufficient to secure a door.

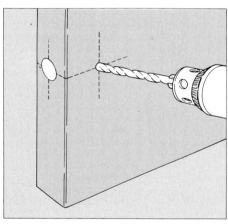

1 Drill a 16mm (⅝in) diameter hole in the door edge for the bolt, and a 10mm diameter hole in the inside face for the key.

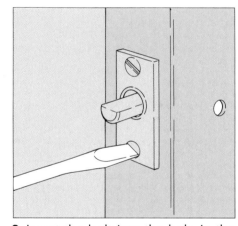

2 Insert the bolt into the hole in the door edge and screw into place. For neatness, recess the faceplate in the door edge.

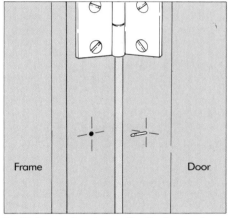

1 Drive pin (supplied) into door edge so it protects by 5mm. Close door and check that the pin has marked the frame.

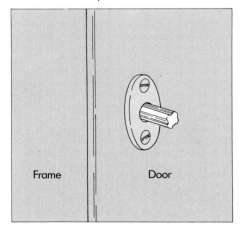

3 Fit the keyhole plate. Close the door and operate the key to mark the position of the locking plate on the frame.

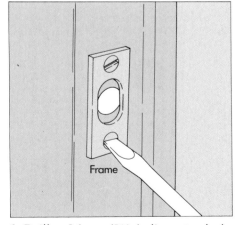

4 Drill a 16mm (⅝in) diameter hole for the bolt engagement and screw faceplate into place. For neatness recess the locking plate.

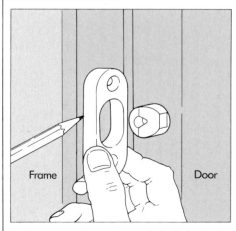

2 Remove the pin and drill hole for bolt which is fitted as shown. Mark outline of the lock plate on frame and cut recess.

Doorchain

Barge-in intruders are not un-known, especially with the elderly, women living alone, and where children have been left by themselves. To deal with this type of threat, either a doorchain or a door limiter should be fitted to the door.

When engaged, doorchains restrict the amount a door can be opened to about 50mm (2in). The traditional type is fixed to a staple mounted on the door frame and the other end is fixed to a button which runs in a metal slot fixed to the door. Some types have a key-operated lock-able staple on the door frame which allows the chain to be used as an extra security device when leaving the house. On return, the door can be opened sufficiently to allow the chain to be unlocked from the staple.

For narrow stile doors, where it would be impossible to fit a slot-type chain-restraint, a chain which runs through a metal loop screwed to the door is available.

Not all chains are really strong and it may be better to fit a high-security device such as a door limiter which is a robust metal sliding catch.

Barrel bolt

It is a good idea to fit bolts at the top and bottom of a door for use at night. The barrel bolt, and the closely related tower bolt, is a surface-mounted bolt which is cheap and easy to fit. The black-painted type is rather unsightly, but there are smaller and more attractive brass and chromium-plated versions ideal for internal doors. The weak point of all these bolts is the staple. It is best to dispense with this and mount the bolt vertically so it shoots directly into holes drilled in the sill and head of the frame.

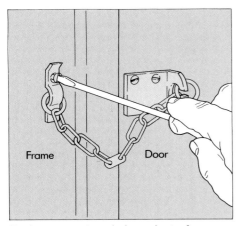

1 A conventional doorchain for narrow stile doors has a staple screwed to the door frame and a ring plate fixed to the door face.

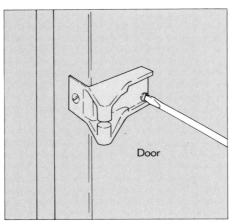

2 To fit a door limiter, fit the guide centrally on the door edge. Cut a recess for the guide to allow the door to close.

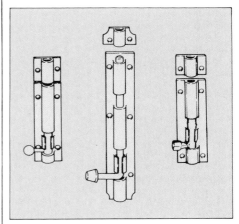

1 Barrel bolts, left and right, have a long guide, while tower bolts, centre, have short ones. Brass and chrome tower bolts are more attractive.

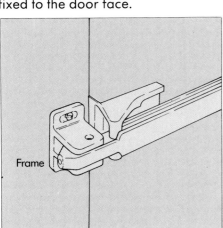

3 Locate the staple on the frame in such a position that the bar will engage freely in the guide but keep the opening distance to a minimum.

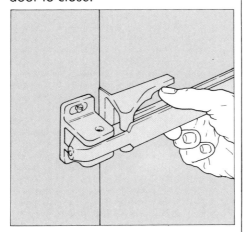

4 Screw the staple to the frame and open the door to check operation of the limiter. Close the door to release the bar.

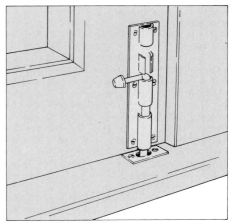

2 Where possible, mount bolts so they shoot into the head and sill of the frame and dispense with the staple.

Intercoms

Even at home you cannot be certain that you are safe from personal attack from an intruder who may just barge in after knocking or ringing the door bell for entry. Of course, those most at risk from this type of incident are the elderly, women living alone, and children who may have been left alone for a few hours. Flat dwellers are often at risk from this type of intrusion too.

Apart from telling children never to answer the door when you are not at home, you can reduce the risk of this type of incident by fitting an intercom and a door viewer to the

1 & 2 Indoor and outdoor units of a door intercom system; 3 A transformer avoids the need for batteries; 4 Receiver and transmitter of a baby-listening intercom that simply plug into 13 amp ring main sockets without the need for connecting wires.

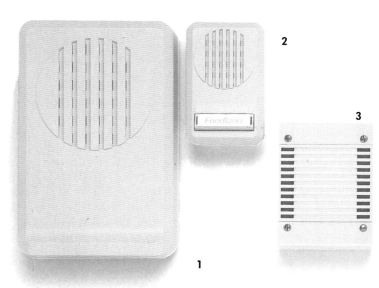

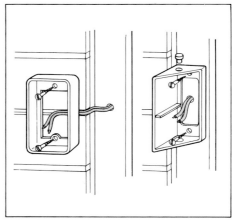

1

2

3

Intercoms work from a low-voltage transformer connected to a three-pin socket or wired into a lighting circuit or ring circuit. Components of this system are connected by bell wire; others require multicore flex. Always follow the manufacturer's instructions.

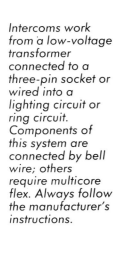

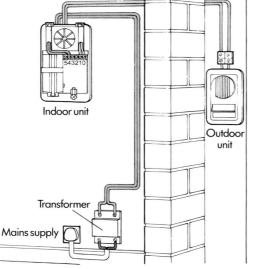

Indoor unit

Outdoor unit

Transformer

Mains supply

1 Drill the door frame and feed through the bell wire into a wall- or corner-mounted bracket.

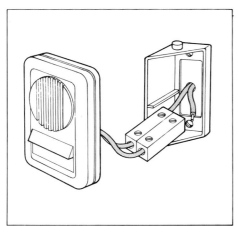

2 Strip 3mm of insulation from the bell wire cores and connect to the terminal block on the outdoor unit. Fix it to the bracket.

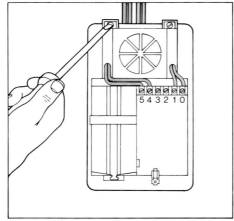

3 Run the bell wire to the indoor unit and run another length to the transformer. Connect both cables to the terminal block in the unit.

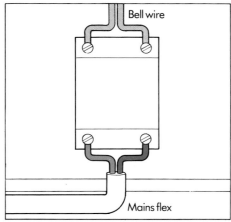

Bell wire

Mains flex

4 Connect the bell wire to the low-voltage transformer terminals, 0.5mm^2 flex runs from the mains terminals to a 3-amp-fused plug.

4

front door so that you can vet callers before opening the door. You will also need a door chain, of course – see page 23.

An intercom system linked to the front door bell enables visitors to be interviewed and identified without opening the door. You can also look at callers through a door viewer. Even more sophisticated is an electronic system of intercom combined with a video camera and small TV monitor.

Yet another option is to fit an entryphone system, which is common in blocks of flats. This allows you to talk to callers at the door, and open the door from a remote point by means of an automatic latch opener.

Entryphones are really useful for the elderly and disabled of course, but they are also useful in detached houses which may be protected with high walls or fences, and secure gates. In this case, to prevent strangers wandering around the garden, you can install an intercom at the gate, so you only have to unlock the gate for bona fide visitors, or you can admit them by fitting an automatic door opener.

Most entryphone kits comprise a low-voltage transformer which powers an intercom handset, with a speaker/receiver and push button unit for mounting at the door, and an optional automatic solenoid-operated latch release which allows you to keep the existing door lock.

Door viewers

Door viewers are ideal for anyone of a nervous disposition because they allow you to check on callers without opening the door – face-to-face contact is avoided and you have the advantage of knowing who is outside without their being able to tell anything about the person inside.

It is very difficult to see in through a viewer, and most models have an internal flap which makes it impossible. With the cover closed it is even impossible to tell whether there is a light on indoors.

A door viewer is like a miniature telescope with a very wide angle of view which is fitted in a door at eye level. The image is rather distorted, but at least you can tell who is at the door. Most door viewers have a field of view of about 160°. It needs to be as wide as possible so that it is impossible for an accomplice to press himself against the wall beside the door without being seen. In the hallway of a block of flats a strategically placed mirror may prevent this. So that callers can be seen at night, a good light outside the door is essential.

Fitting a door viewer simply involves drilling a hole of about 13mm diameter in the door. It is best in the middle of the door at eye height – not too high or children or the elderly may not be able to use it, and not too low or you will not be able to see clearly the face of callers. Most door viewers are in two parts which screw together and therefore cope with a wide range of door thicknesses; from 25mm to 59mm is normal.

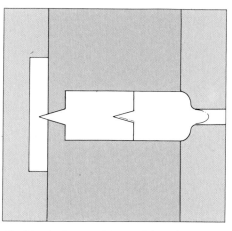

1 Mark the position of the viewer on outside of door. Drill through into scrap wood to prevent splintering.

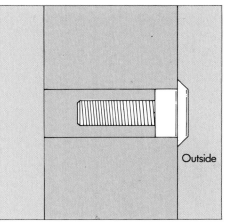

Outside

2 Position the outside section of the viewer (identified from the manufacturer's instructions).

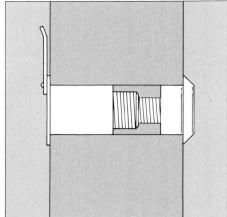

3 From inside, screw in the other part (with the cover, if fitted); hand-tighten the two together.

DOOR FRAME

You can have the best door locks and bolts in the world, but if your door or door frame is weak, they will be useless.

Check external door frames for rot, especially close to the base where the posts (uprights) are jointed into the sill. Check that the joints are not broken and make sure the frame is firmly fixed in the opening. If it is loose, refix it by drilling through the frame into the brickwork at the sides and inserting purpose-made frame-fixing devices.

The door itself should also be checked for rot and weak joints.

Removing an old door and frame

If the hinge screw slots are filled with paint, scrape this out and then, while holding the screwdriver blade in the slot, strike the screwdriver handle sharply.

To remove a rotted frame, cut through one of the posts (also called jambs) using an old saw. Lever this post away from the wall then lever down the head of the frame, followed by the other post and sill.

Fitting a new frame

Buy a frame which is a tight fit in the opening. For a non-standard size opening, a new frame and door will have to be made to measure.

Check that the dpc (the damp-proof 'course' of bitumen or plastic strip) is intact at the base. If necessary, bed a new strip of dpc on cement mortar, then position the frame and wedge it in place so that the head and sill are level, the posts are upright, and the diagonals are of equal length which indicates that the frame is square. Also place a spirit level on the front and back faces of the posts to ensure that the frame is upright in the opening.

Drill through the frame uprights at three places on each side to coincide with the mid-points of whole bricks. If you use frame-fixing devices drill through the fixing holes into the brickwork which will allow

1 Remove the old door then saw through the frame jambs, angling the saw cuts slightly.

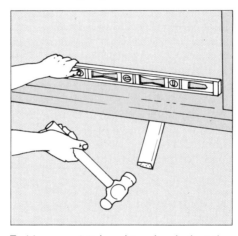

5 Use a spirit level to check that the sill is level. Temporarily wedge under the sill if necessary.

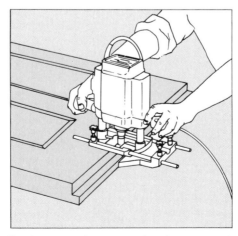

9 Cut a rebate in the bottom of a door using a router. The rebate closes against a water bar in the sill.

2 Lever out the frame sections using a wrecking bar. A batten under the lever will protect the brickwork.

6 Next check that the jambs are vertical on all faces. If necessary use thin timber wedges to achieve this.

10 Holding the door against the frame, run a pencil around the frame to mark the face of the door.

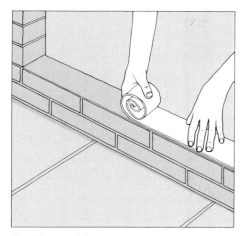

3 Clean old mortar out of the opening, then prepare the base by laying a strip of dpc on cement mortar.

4 Lay a thin strip of mortar over the dpc, then fit the new frame taking care not to displace the dpc.

7 Bore holes through the frame and into the brickwork, then drive in the frame-fixing devices and tighten.

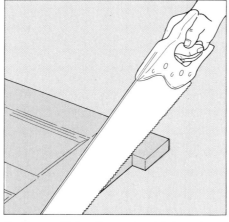

8 Saw off the 'horns', which protect the door in transit, flush with the top and bottom rails of the door.

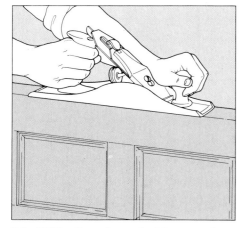

11 With the door held on edge, plane down to the marked line. A slight bevel will prevent binding.

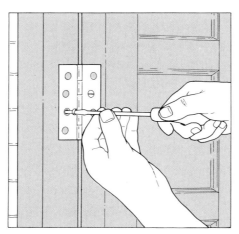

12 Cut the recesses, fit the hinges temporarily with one screw per side, and try the operation of the door.

the frame-fixers to be inserted and tightened up without having to remove the frame again. If you are using conventional screws and wall-plugs for fixing, the frame must be removed and holes drilled for wall-plugs at the marked fixing-hole positions. Insert wallplugs, then replace the frame, checking that it is square and upright, and screw it into place.

Hanging a new door

If the door is supplied with protective 'horns', cut these off. While a helper holds the door steady against the frame, mark around it on the face of the door to give a gap of about 2mm (1/16 in) all round the edge.

Remove the door and while holding it on edge, plane down to the pencil line. If there is a lot of wood to remove it will be quicker to saw along the door as close to the trimming line as possible, then finish by planing. When planing the top or bottom edges of the door, work from the ends towards the middle of the rail to avoid splitting the wood.

With external doors, the threshold (step) of the frame is fitted with a water bar and the bottom of the door must be rebated to fit over it. The rebate can be cut using a router, or a circular saw can be set to the depth of the rebate and the waste chiselled away.

To fit hinges, position the door in the opening on packing pieces to give the correct clearance at the base. If fitting a new door into an existing frame, mark the hinge recess positions on the edge of the door. If both frame and door are new, mark hinge positions on door and frame; they are set 150–175mm (6–7in) from the top and 200–250mm (8–10in) up from the bottom. Cut out the hinge flap recesses and fit the hinges to the door using one screw per hinge for the time being.

Wedge the door in the open position and fit the hinges to the frame with one screw per hinge, then check the operation of the door before fitting all the screws. These should be a minimum of 38mm (1½in) long and large gauge, but must sit flush.

WINDOWS

Windows are particularly weak spots in the home defence, but they are easily protected. All ground-floor windows should be fitted with secure key-operated locks and similar locks should also be fitted to upstairs windows, particularly those which are accessible. Burglars often break a small pane to allow a hand through to open a catch. A window lock will prevent his, but you need to be sure that there is at least one window in each room that you can open quickly from inside in case of fire. This means keeping the key accessible but well out of reach and sight of the window.

TIMBER CASEMENTS

Timber casements may be hinged at the side (side-hung), in the middle (pivoting), or at the top (top-hung), which is frequently the case with fanlights.

It is these smaller windows which are often the biggest security risk. You should never leave them open, even when leaving the house for a short time.

Always close and lock all windows when leaving the house. Improve the security of ground-floor windows which are out of view from the road and neighbouring properties.

Such windows need key-operated locks which are screwed tightly in place to prevent them from being opened if the catch is forced. Most windows will need only one lock, but large windows will need two.

One of the most popular locks for timber casement windows is the window mortise rack bolt. Like the door bolt, the window rack bolt is fitted into the edge of the casement

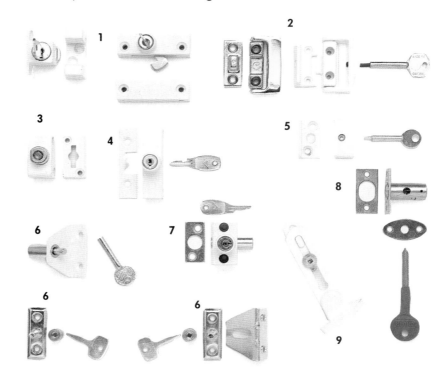

1 Catch-type locks; 2 Hinged locks; 3 Push-bolt lock; 4 Self-locking lock; 5 Screw lock; 6 Stay bolt and screw-down stay locks; 7 Key-operated bolt; 8 Mortise security bolt; 9 Child safety stay.

FITTING A MORTISE RACK BOLT

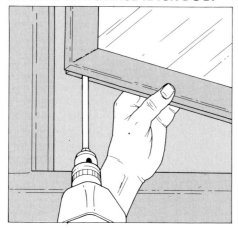

1 Drill a hole in the casement frame to accommodate the body of the rack bolt.

2 Cut a recess in the frame so the face plate is flush with the surface. Screw the bolt in place.

3 Close window and wind out bolt to mark frame. Drill a hole here to accept the bolt. Fit a cover plate.

FITTING A CASEMENT WINDOW LOCK

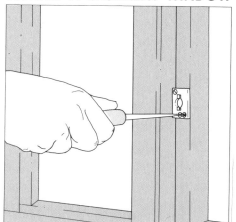

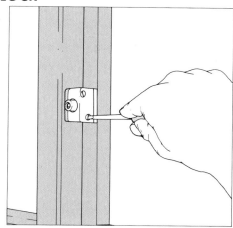

1 Mark the position of the lock on the casement and the frame. Screw the backplate to the casement.

2 Fit the lock on to the backplate and if the frame is tapered, fit a wedge between lock and the frame.

3 Screw the lock to the side of the frame; cover screw holes with plastic plugs supplied. Test.

frame. A serrated key is used to wind the bolt out into the frame. The key is removed after use and the bolt cannot be pushed back into the lock without it. With a small side-hung window, one lock close to the centre of the frame will be sufficient, but a larger window will need two, one near the top of the window, and one near the bottom. For a top-hung casement fit two rack bolts, one on each side close to the bottom.

Another way of securing top-hung casements is to fit window-stay locks. They can be used to hold the

window in its closed position or they can be locked while the window is slightly open, but they do not prevent the stay from being sawn through or unscrewed, so they are best used in addition to rack bolts, or as a safety precaution to prevent young children from climbing out.

There are several types of window-stay locks. A common type replaces one of the existing casement-stay pegs with a threaded peg. The stay is held in place with a locknut that can be removed only with a special key. For stays without

holes for the fixing peg, a casement-stay bolt can be used.

A good lock for side-hung casements and top-hung casements is the casement window lock. There are various types, some of which lock automatically when the window is closed; all are key-operated and simply screw to the opening casement frame and to the fixed frame.

A robust lock for side, top-hung and pivoting casements is the hinged window lock. When the window is closed the catch is fixed with a screw operated by a special key.

FITTING WINDOW STAY LOCKS

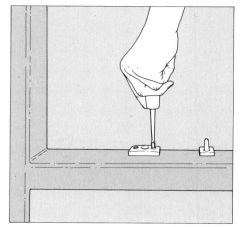

1 Replace one of the casement-stay securing pegs with the window-stay lock. It simply screws to the frame.

2 Close the window then screw down the window-stay lock into the peg using the special key provided.

3 For a stay without holes, fit a window-stay bolt as shown here. The main part screws to the frame.

TIMBER SASHES

In the past, sliding sash windows were notoriously easy to open; inserting a knife blade between the sashes from outside was sufficient to knock back the arm of the fastener, allowing the bottom sash to be lifted for easy entry. To a large extent this problem has been eliminated by fitting up-to-date fasteners, like the fitch fastener which has a snail-like cam that cannot be knocked back, and the Brighton fastener, which has a screw-down acorn that securely clamps the sashes together. Both catches draw the sashes together to help prevent draughts but neither can be considered a security device because the window is still easily opened by breaking a pane of glass which will allow the fastener to be turned back by hand.

A very simple way to prevent a sash window from being opened is to screw the meeting rails of the two sash frames together. If the screw heads are countersunk, filled, and painted, it can be very effective. However, for safety in the event of fire, it is essential that at least one window in each room can be opened quickly, and if the room is large one window on each side of the room. This means fitting proprietary security devices.

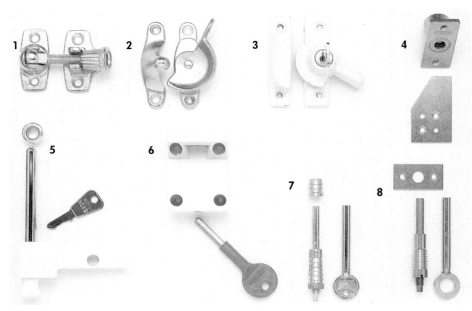

There are basically three types of security devices for sash windows. These are the locking stop, the dual screw, and the sash lock.

The locking stop (also called the acorn stop) is a cheap device which is usually best fitted in pairs; one stop on each side of the window. A metal plate is recessed into the frame upright at each side of the upper sash, just above the meeting rail. The plate is threaded and a metal button (or acorn) is screwed into the plate by means of a special key supplied with the device. The button prevents

1 & 2 Brighton
& fitch catches;
3 Locking fitch;
4 Push-bolt stop;
5 Locking bolt;
6 Clench lock;
7 & 8 Easy-fit &
screw-in dual
screws.

the two sashes from passing each other but can be placed to allow an adequate amount of ventilation without posing a security risk. The locking stops can be removed to allow escape.

Often two fixing plates are positioned at each side of the window giving the option that it can be locked closed or slightly open.

FITTING A LOCKING CATCH

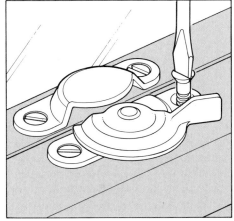

1 Unscrew the existing catch and catch plate from the meeting rails and make good.

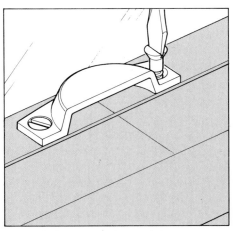

2 Mark the centre line of the meeting rails and screw the catch plate centrally to the outer sash.

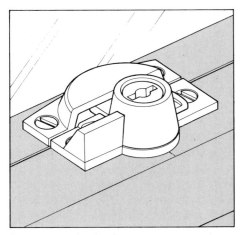

3 Position the locking catch and fasten it to locate it, then screw it to the inner meeting rail.

FITTING A DUAL SCREW

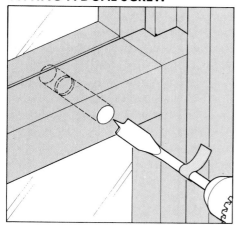

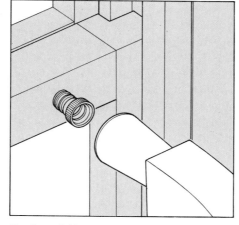

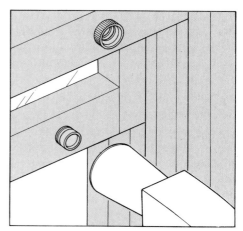

1 Close windows and drill through the top rail of the inner sash into the outer frame to a depth of 15mm.

2 Carefully tap the large barrel (using a plastic mallet) into the inner frame until it lies flush.

3 Open the window and tap the small barrel into the bottom rail of the outer frame.

If you do not require to be able to lock sashes in the open position for ventilation, you may prefer to fit dual screws. These work by securing the meeting rails of the two sashes together, but have a key-operated removable bolt which can be easily unscrewed.

Although both locking stops and dual screws are cheap, the problem with these devices is that they are very slow to operate and this could be a decided disadvantage if anyone needed to make a quick escape – in the case of a fire, for example. On at least one window in a set, therefore, it is worth fitting a key-operated sash window lock.

There are various types of locks. One type which is fairly easy to fit replaces a fitch fastener in the middle of the meeting rails. It has a similar clenching action to a fitch fastener, but the cam is operated by a key and cannot be turned back once the key is removed.

Another easy-fit lock is the sash window press-bolt. Again, the two parts of the lock simply screw on top of the meeting rails and a push-button bolt locks the two parts of the lock together. A simple key is used to unlock the bolt.

There is also a more sophisticated push-button sash window lock which is fixed at one side of the window on the top rail of the lower sash. Pushing a button shoots a bolt into a small hole drilled in the upright of the upper sash. A second hole can be drilled slightly above the first which will allow some ventilation without affecting security. Larger windows require one of these locks to be fitted on each side of the window.

FITTING A SASH WINDOW LOCK

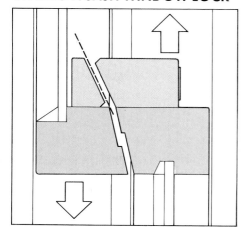

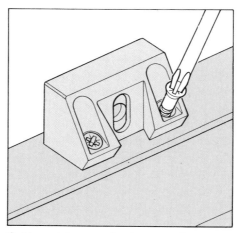

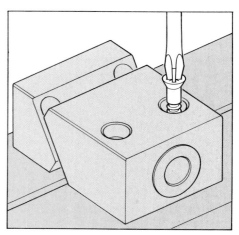

1 This surface-mounted lock has a clenching action when the two parts are secured by the key.

2 Mount the catch plate on the outer sash near the catch, or mount one each side on larger windows.

3 Screw the lock body to the inner sash meeting rail and fit cover plugs over the screws.

METAL WINDOWS

In older houses, metal window frames are usually substantial and are made from steel or galvanized steel. Apart from the difficulty of drilling the frames – you will need a high-speed steel twist-drill bit used at slow speed in an electric drill or hand-drill – fitting security devices to this type of window will improve security considerably.

On the other hand, aluminium-framed windows, such as the type frequently fitted as replacement windows, present special difficulties. They are often fitted with poor-quality locks as standard and because the aluminium alloy used is thin and soft it is difficult to fit many of the standard metal window locks succesfully. The self-tapping (self-threading) screws used tend to pull out easily and a lever will distort the frames allowing easy entry. To some extent the problem can be overcome by gluing the locks to the frames with epoxy resin adhesive in addition to self-tapping screws.

The best advice for aluminium replacement windows is to make sure that they are fitted with security locks in the factory by the manufacturer; look for BS4873.

The type of metal window most commonly found is the steel hinged

FITTING A PIVOTING METAL WINDOW LOCK

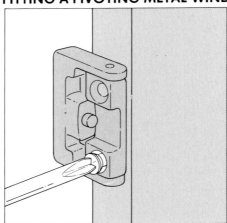

1 Drill fixing holes for the pivoting part of the lock on the opening frame. Screw lock in place.

2 Close the lock with the locking staple in place, then mark the fixing holes on the frame.

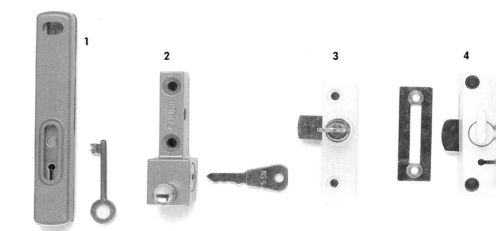

1   2   3   4

FITTING A SLIDING BOLT COCKSPUR HANDLE BOLT

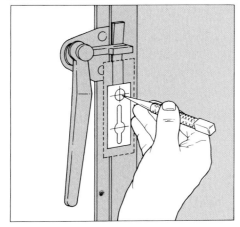

1 Hold the template on the frame just below the handle and mark the hole positions with a centre punch.

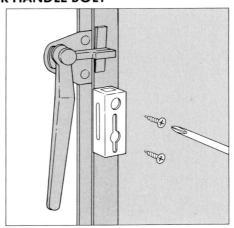

2 Carefully drill the frame and fit the lock body with self-tapping screws which are provided.

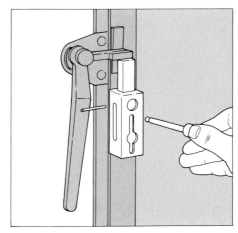

3 Insert the bolt according to manufacturer's instructions. Test the action of the lock with the key supplied.

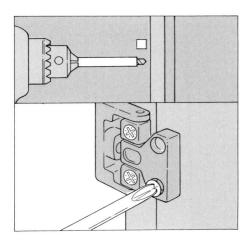

3 With a depth stop on the drill, make the fixing holes and screw the staple in place.

casement. The small top light (or fanlight) is usually top-hung and can be held in various positions to regulate ventilation by means of a stay of some sort – usually a pin stay or peg stay. The ventilation bar or stay is also used to hold the window closed by clipping alongside the pins or pegs. Similar stays are used to control ventilation in side-opening casements, and variations on the theme include telescopic and sliding stays, but a handle known as a cockspur fastener is used to hold the window closed.

Security devices for metal windows tend to be locks to hold the ventilation stay closed and locks to prevent the cockspur handle from being opened.

Casement stay locks – These are very simple clamp-on devices which hold casement ventilation stays in the closed position. They should be key-operated so they are not easily removed by an intruder. Another type is the key-operated casement lock which has a swinging or sliding bar which prevents the arm from being lifted off the retainer.

Cockspur handle bolt – This key-operated lock attaches to the fixed part of the frame, just below the cockspur handle, and prevents the handle from being opened.

Metal window lock – Various key-operated surface-fitting locks are available. The lock is fitted by means of self-tapping screws to the opening edge of the window frame, as near the centre as possible. Turning a catch operates the swinging bolt which locks against the fixed part of the frame. The bolt is released by a key.

Another type is a pivoting lock where the hinged catch is fitted on to the opening frame and it locks on to a staple fitted to the fixed frame by means of a simple screw-down key.

Fitting locks of this type is quite difficult because it involves drilling steel. Use a centre punch to make a dimple in the metal to stop the drill bit from skidding across the frame as each hole is started.

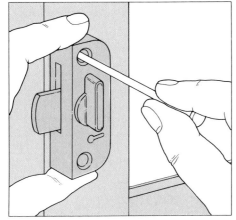

1 Sliding cockspur-handle lock; 2 Sliding metal window lock; 3 Key-operated lock; 4 Locking handle-operated catch; 5 Hinged lock; 6 Stay stops.

FITTING A CATCH AND KEY-OPERATED LOCK (Chubb 8K100)

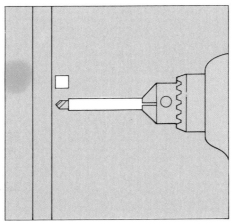

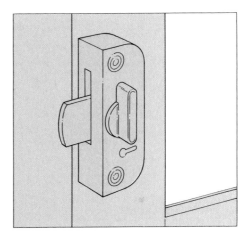

1 Position the lock on the opening frame to give maximum engagement of the bolt on the fixed frame.

2 Fit a depth stop to the recommended twist bit and drill the holes. Large windows need two locks.

3 Screw the lock in place using the self-tapping screws supplied. Seal the screw holes with plastic plugs.

SLIDING WINDOWS

In most cases horizontal sliding windows will be made from aluminium sliding on an aluminium track. Security devices for this type of window should prevent the window from being forced open when closed, or from being lifted out of its track.

A good device is a key-operated sliding window lock. It screws on to the edge of the inside window and a protruding bolt allows it to be locked to the outer pane. This type of lock is popular for securing patio doors, but the window frame might not be wide enough, in which case fit a clamp-on type of lock. This is attached to the sliding track with the window in the closed position. Both types can also be used on vertical sliding metal windows.

For securing horizontal-sliding timber windows, a useful device is the dual screw, as used for timber vertical-sliding sash windows. Some types of bolt window locks can also be used on horizontal sliding sash windows.

PATIO DOORS

There is very little that can be done to improve the security of sliding aluminium or plastic patio doors as security depends on the quality of the original equipment fitted by the manufacturer. So check the door carefully before buying to satisfy yourself that secure locks are fitted.

If you have an existing patio door with doubtful security, it will be necessary to fit substantial sliding door locks to the top and bottom of the fixed frame.

FRENCH WINDOWS

French windows are normally hinged, double doors that open outwards. They are often vulnerable from a security point of view because they are glazed and not overlooked. Security can be improved dramatically by changing ordinary window glass to toughened or laminated.

To a large extent, security with metal-framed French windows is dependent on the quality of the locks fitted by the manufacturer. However, security can usually be improved by fitting the bolting door of the pair with key-operated metal-window bolts at the top and bottom. The door with the latch should also have two bolts close to the top and bottom.

Timber French windows are even more vulnerable, often because they are weakened by wood rot. If they are badly decayed, new doors should be fitted.

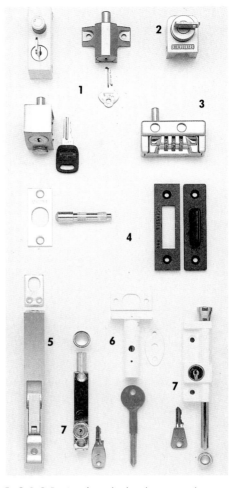

1, 2 & 3 Patio-door bolt, clamp and combination locks; *4* Hinge bolt; *5* Flush bolt; *6* Mortise security bolt; *7* Locking bolt.

FITTING A SLIDING WINDOW/DOOR LOCK

1 Decide on the best place to fit the lock. It must not interfere with the rolling gear or the glass.

2 The usual position is on the edge of the inner door. Fix the mounting plate with three self-tapping screws.

3 Slide lock on to mounting plate and screw in place. Operate to mark frame and drill 10mm hole for bolt.

FITTING HINGE BOLTS

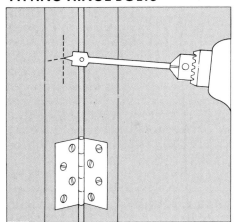

1 Drill the edge of the door at a convenient position within about 75mm of the top and bottom hinges.

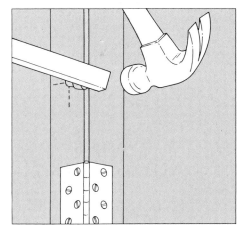

2 Drive the hinge bolt into the hole using a piece of wood to prevent the bolt from being damaged.

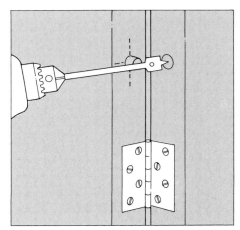

3 Partially close the door so that the bolt marks the frame, then drill the frame to accept the hinge bolt.

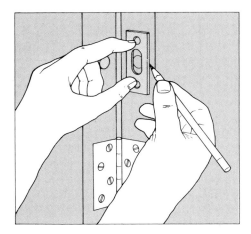

4 Hold the lock plate over the hole and mark round its outline on to the frame.

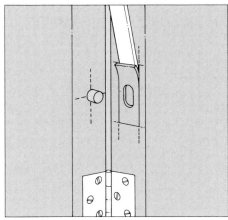

5 Chisel out a recess for the plate in the edge of the frame so the plate lies flush with the surface.

6 Position the lock plate and screw it into place. Test that the door operates smoothly.

Sound timber French windows need good rack bolts at top and bottom. Fit flush bolts in the rebate of the second-opening door and mortise rack bolts to the first-opening door, shooting into the head and sill of the frame. Where the pair of doors meet, fit a mortise deadlock or a hook-bolt mortise lock.

In some older houses French windows are secured with an espagnolette bolt which extends the full length of the door and consists of two sliding bolts, operated by a central handle. The handle should be lockable. If it is not a deadlocking mortise lock should be fitted, together with mortise rack bolts at the top and bottom of both doors.

A big problem with outward-opening doors is that the hinge pins can be knocked out and the doors prised open on the hinge side. This can be prevented by fitting hinge bolts in the hinge edge of the door, close to the hinge positions, as described on page 22.

LOUVRE WINDOWS

Louvre windows present special problems from the security point of view. With the cheaper types it is a simple matter for an intruder to re-move whole strips of glass from the metal clips.

It is best not to fit louvre windows on the ground floor or where they are easily accessible. If they are already fitted, consider changing them or covering them with fixed metal security grilles.

Modern, good-quality louvre windows now have fixed louvres or locking devices.

To improve the security of existing louvres, you can change the louvre blades to the laminated safety glass type and glue the blades into their holders using strong epoxy resin adhesive.

DOUBLE GLAZING

In itself, double glazing does not make a window more secure: what it does mean is that an intruder has another pane of glass to break in order to force an entry. This in turn means more noise, and more time spent in breaking in.

The security value of double glazing depends on the type of double glazing fitted, on the type of locks fitted to the windows, and on the glazing material used and the system in the case of secondary double glazing.

There is no doubt that double glazing is a deterrent to an intruder, and coupled with its other benefits, such as energy conservation, you have several good reasons to install it in your home.

The benefits of double glazing are well established. It will reduce heat loss through single glazed windows by half, and as 10–15 per cent on average is lost through the windows, by completely double glazing a house you could save up to 5 per cent of your fuel bills.

There are many other reasons, not least the security aspect, which make fitting double glazing worthwhile. It will eliminate draughts to make the whole floor area of a room usable on cold days, and the 'greenhouse effect' will boost room temperatures on sunny winter days.

Condensation will also be reduced and possibly eliminated in rooms that are double glazed, correctly heated and ventilated. Condensation occurs when warm, moist air inside the room contacts a cold window pane and frame. With double glazing the inner pane of glass will be warmer, and therefore less prone to misting over.

Noise will be considerably reduced by any form of double glazing using glass, but if the problem is excessive, it should be tailor-made for noise reduction. This means making the gap between the inner and the outer panes at least 100mm (4in) and ideally 200mm (8in). Also, the panes of glass in the window and in the secondary glazing should be of different thicknesses to ensure that sound waves passing between one pane and another are not amplified. In cases where the noise problem is very serious it may be possible to get a grant to install double glazing – inquire at your local government offices.

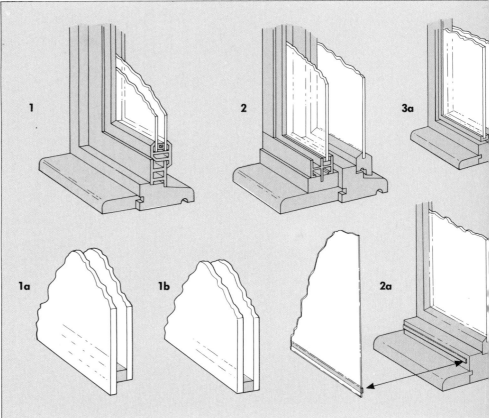

Condensation

The solution to the perennial problem of condensation depends on where it forms. For example, misting on the room side does not indicate a fault with the double glazing at all; just that the temperature of the glass is too low given the water content of the air in the room. The only solution in this case is to strike a balance between adequate heating and ventilation.

Condensation on the surface of the glass within the cavity usually indicates that moisture-laden air is leaking into the cavity from within the room. With secondary double glazing the solution is to seal around the glazing panel as thoroughly as possible in an attempt to make it airtight. Try to do this on a warm, dry day. If this fails to cure the problem, try drilling ventilation holes through the outer window frame to the outside air. The holes should be about 10mm (3/8in) in diameter and slope downwards towards the outside to prevent rain from entering. They should also be plugged with glassfibre wool to prevent insects from crawling inside. The number of holes required will be a matter of trial and error, but as a guide, for a window about 1m (3ft) wide, two holes spaced 500mm (18in) apart will suffice. Larger windows need more holes pro rata. Alternatively, sachets of silica gel crystals placed in the void between the panes will absorb any moisture.

In theory, condensation cannot occur between the panes in hermetically sealed units because air in the cavity is dried and the air gap is totally sealed, but sometimes the problem does occur, due either to ficult to break, window security depends on the quality of the locks fitted by the window manufacturer. Adding additional security locks later is unlikely to be a viable proposition, so make sure the windows pane of glass is larger than the inner one so that the unit is stepped and will fit into the rebate.

Sealed units give you all the thermal insulation benefits of double glazing, but as with replacement windows, while the glass itself presents more of a challenge to the intruder, security of the windows is only as good as their locks.

Secondary glazing is the type of double glazing that is most commonly fitted. It comprises a separate pane of glass or plastic fitted to the inside of an existing window frame. The secondary glazing panel can be fixed, which is acceptable for non-opening windows, or it can be easily opened, which is the type required for windows used constantly.

From the security point of view, it is the glass-glazed systems that are preferable to the plastic types since breaking a pane of glass makes more noise and is more dangerous than breaking a sheet of plastic. However, secondary systems that use thick sheets of acrylic plastic form quite a tough barrier (polycarbonate is 250 times stronger than glass!) as long as they are securely fixed. With any type of openable secondary glazing system, security, as before, is only as good as the locks fitted to hold the glazing closed.

Temporary double glazing systems are now widely available. Most are easy to fit and are effective at reducing heat loss, but they have no value as far as providing additional security. There are three main types – magnetic, clip-on, and clear plastic film which shrinks tight when heated using a hairdryer.

1 Sealed double-glazing units may be stepped (1a) or square-edged (1b); 2 A typical secondary system has horizontal sliding sashes. They may also be magnetic (2a), hinged (2b) or slide vertically (2c). Secondary sashes are fixed to the opening casement (3a), the fixed frame (3b) or the reveal (3c).

faulty manufacture in the case of a new window, or due to a gradual breakdown of the seal in the case of an older window. Unfortunately, when seal breakdown occurs, the only solution is to replace the units with new ones.

Types of double glazing

There are basically four types of double glazing – replacement windows, sealed units, secondary sashes, and temporary systems.

Replacement windows are supplied made-to-measure to fit your window opening. They are supplied with hermetically sealed glazing units which makes them efficient thermal insulators, but although the glazing units themselves may be dif-

are fitted with secure locks – ideally with locking concealed bolts that shoot into both the head and sill of the frame.

Provided the existing window frames are sound, you can retain them and simply replace the glass with sealed units. In this case, each window is fitted with a factory-made hermetically sealed unit comprising two pieces of glass which are fused together at the edges with a small air space between the panes. The unit simply fits into the frame as a normal sheet of glass. However, with most existing frames, the glass rebate will not be deep enough to accept a normal straight-edged sealed unit, so a stepped unit will have to be specified. In this case the outer

Shutters

Although not a double glazing system as such, window shutters are valuable for conserving heat loss through the windows when they are closed. Both internally fitted and externally fitted shutters are excellent security devices as long as they are lockable from the inside. Obviously, they are only useful at night. If shutters are closed during the day this is a sure sign that the

FITTING PVC HORIZONTAL SLIDING UNITS

1 Measure the window recess and cut the outer frames accurately.

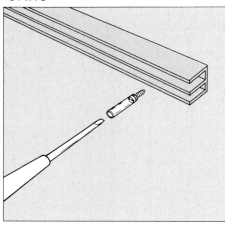

2 A screw-guide in the kit locates screws in deep channels.

3 Screw the tracks to the frames and then measure up for the glass and framing channels.

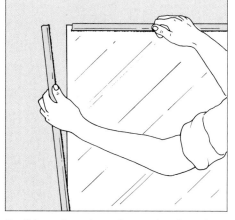

4 Glass framing channel is fitted on to the edges of the glass (or acrylic or polycarbonate) sheets.

5 Lift the framed glazing panels into the tracks and check that they slide smoothly.

6 Finally, fit self-adhesive handles, together with additional security locks if required.

house is unoccupied and could encourage a burglar to force an entry through another route, such as a door or unguarded window.

Secondary glazing kits

Secondary glazing kits that will improve security, as well as providing thermal insulation, comprise a framework made from plastic or aluminium channel strips in which the glass or rigid plastic sheets are fixed.

The simplest systems use U-shaped soft plastic channel which is mitred at the corners and fitted around a pane of glass. The assembly is held against the window and is fixed to the frame using small plastic clips. The system is cheap, but for cleaning the glass panel has to be unclipped completely which is inconvenient and time-consuming. Fixed windows can be enclosed completely, which will eliminate draughts, but if the window opens, the secondary panel must be attached to the opening frame. This will reduce heat loss through the window, but it will not eliminate draughts from around the edge of the frame and for security you still rely on the effectiveness of the window locks.

More elaborate hinged or fixed secondary glazing systems are much more effective. This type consists of substantial plastic or aluminium channel which is cut to length and joined at the corners by mitring, or by using special corner joiners supplied in the kit. The secondary glazing panels can be hinged to open sideways or upwards to match the hinging of the casements over which they are hung. This type is superior to the system previously mentioned in that, if correctly assembled, the glazing panel will completely eliminate draughts, and if fitted with secure locks, will also improve security.

The fixed-pane system is mainly for use on smaller, fixed or seldom opened windows – up to about 1200mm (48in) high by 700mm (28in) wide. If possible, choose the type that can be fitted inside the window

FITTING A PVC VERTICAL SLIDING SASH UNIT

1 Measure the height of the window recess and cut the side tracks to fit.

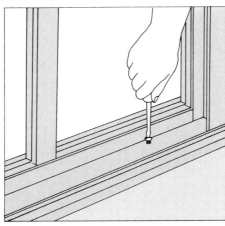

2 Cut the top and bottom tracks and fit around the side tracks each end.

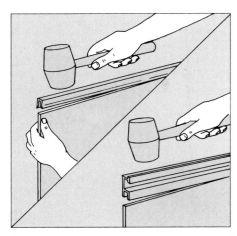

3 Measure and cut the glass, stand it on folded newspapers or cloth and tap the edging strip into place.

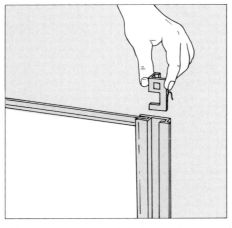

4 Fit a sash catch into each end of the lower section ensuring the wire hooks are under the bottom edge.

5 Press the ratchet sash guides into the side tracks until they click into position, then fit the sliding panes.

6 Lift the upper (outer) then the inner sash into the guides so that the catches engage.

recess with side tracks that allow it to be lifted out easily for cleaning.

Unlike sliding systems (see below) hinged secondary glazing systems do not need an outer track. Instead, channel (usually aluminium) frames the glass, and hinges, catches and stays are then fitted to the window surround, and the glazed frame is lifted into place. There is a limit to the size of hinged secondary units – usually 1.1sq m (about 12sq ft) when side hinged, and 1.7sq m (about 18sq ft) when top hinged – so for larger windows, fit several hinged panels.

Sliding systems are a little more complicated to fit as they involve two separate frames, but they are very effective both for thermal insulation and improved security. Because the glass is well supported in these systems, they are more suitable for large windows than hinged types. Horizontal and vertical sliding units are available. With the horizontal sliding system, the panes run in tracks fixed to the inside of the window recess. The panes are easily opened for ventilation (or escape in case of emergency), and they can be lifted out for cleaning. Horizontal sliders are suitable for windows up to about 2.2sq m (24sq ft). Two frames are required – one fits on to the window surround or in the window recess, and the other is made up to fit around the glass pane. The glazed frame fits into the frame fixed to the window surround.

Vertical sliding secondary glazing systems are designed for vertical sliding sash windows, but can be used on most windows where access is required to the top or bottom of the window. Like horizontal sliding glazing systems, vertical sliding systems consist of two frames which slide vertically to open or close. Usually there are finger catches to hold the frames in any position. Most systems are suitable for windows up to about 2.4m high by 1.2m wide (8 × 4ft), but no single pane should exceed 1.1sq m (12sq ft). The outer frame can usually be fitted inside the window recess, or to the flat timber window surround.

ALARM SYSTEMS

More and more householders are installing burglar alarms. They are not a substitute for good locks on doors and windows, but they are an excellent adjunct to them, and a bell box or siren fitted high up on an outside wall is a prominent deterrent to a would-be burglar. An alarm is there only to alert that someone has entered. With the alarm sound-ing, the hope is that the burglar will quickly leave.

When you are choosing a burglar alarm system, consider your needs, and make sure that the alarm is capable of meeting these requirements. Although alarms are becoming increasingly sophisticated, not all systems that are available are of top quality, including some offered for D-I-Y installation.

There are several good reasons for fitting a burglar alarm. For example, in itself the alarm box on the outside of the house is a strong visual indication that you have taken security precautions and prob-ably have good locks fitted in addi-tion to an alarm. This may be suffi-cient to deter a would-be thief.

Another benefit of an alarm is that as soon as the alarm sounds it is likely that the thief will leave, and hopefully this will be before he has even broken into the house (as he opens a protected window or door, say); or if he has gained entry, the alarm should persuade him to leave before he has had time to make a search or do a lot of damage.

Most systems provide a panic but-ton which will sound the alarm when-ever the button is pressed, whether the alarm is in use or not, and this can be reassuring at night or when anyone is left in the house alone. Some systems also incorporate a smoke detector.

Some people refuse to have an alarm because they feel it shows would-be thieves that there is some-thing worth stealing in the house, although this argument is not so convincing now that burglar alarms are much more commonly fitted.

Another argument against having an alarm is the number of false alarms they can give. This can be a nuisance by disturbing neighbours and if there are too many false alarms, soon no one takes any notice even if the alert is a genuine one.

Choosing an alarm

When it comes to choosing an alarm system for D-I-Y installation you can either go for an alarm kit, or you can make up a system by buying

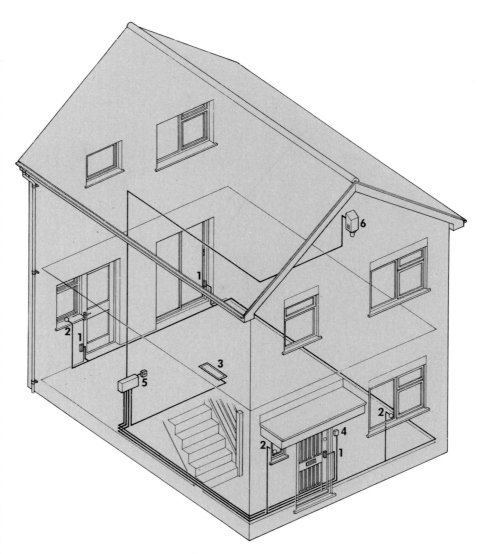

Above: Typical layout of a simple single-zone burglar alarm system protecting the vulnerable ground-floor entry points.

Right: Layout of a two-zone system in a similar house. One zone protects all the vulnerable entry points on the ground and first floors, while the second zone connects the internal doors and pressure pads to locate an intruder as he moves about the house. At night, only the first zone is activated, allowing the family to move about inside the house without triggering the alarm.

1 Door sensor	**2** Window sensor
3 Pressure mat	**4** Panic button
5 Control unit	**6** External sounder

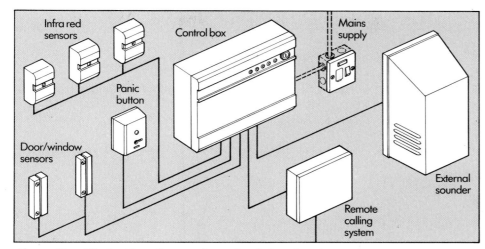

Above: Simplified wiring diagram for a simple burglar alarm system.

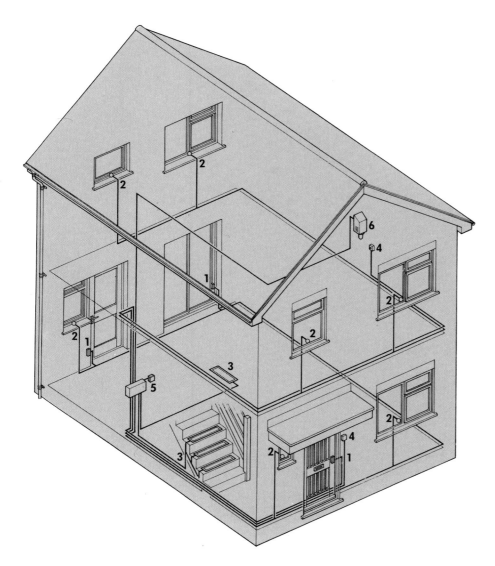

individual components and cable.

By doing it yourself, rather than opting for a professional installation, you will save a lot of money. The job is not difficult: kits are supplied with full and comprehensive fitting instructions. However, you will be a little more on your own if you buy the components individually. Even so, most components are supplied with a wiring diagram, at the very least. It will probably take a couple of weekends to install a burglar alarm system.

Types of D-I-Y alarm

Burglar alarms for D-I-Y fitting tend to be one of two types. The traditional type has circuits that link door and window sensors of various types, and pressure detectors, to a central control box which in turn is linked to the alarm box, which may be a bell, siren, flashing light, or even a remote calling system which automatically dials a preprogrammed telephone number to raise the alarm. The door and window sensors are magnetic switches that detect when the door or window is opened, while the pressure detectors are pads placed on the floor under carpets at strategic points. The former are usually more useful because they are designed to prevent entry.

The second type of alarm is the sophisticated electronic type which detects the presence of an intruder by means of infrared detectors which pick up body heat, or ultrasonic detectors which pick up movement. These electronic alarms often incorporate features such as window and door sensors that are found in traditional alarm systems.

The sophisticated electronic type of alarm is not usually available in kit form, and you would have to make this up from components.

When choosing a kit, make sure that the alarm is sufficiently loud — it should be at least 95 decibels. Also check the quality of the components and make sure that the alarm box cannot be removed without triggering the alarm.

Control unit

The central part is the control unit which allows you to set the alarm, switch it off, and decide how much of the system is to be activated. It also provides a power supply for the system and keeps a constant check on the sensors, activating the alarm if the sensors are tampered with, or if it detects a change in the signals sent to it, caused by the presence of an intruder.

Most control units also have a facility for testing the system which verifies that the system is working and alerts you if any doors or windows are open, or other detectors are in an open position.

Once the control unit has told you that the system is functioning correctly, the unit can be turned on using a key, or a simple number code which is typed into a keypad on the control unit.

There is an exit delay feature which allows you to set the control unit and get out of the house without setting off the alarm, and similarly there should be an entry delay which allows you to walk in and switch off the control unit before the alarm is sounded.

The control unit must be carefully sited so that it is not immediately accessible to an intruder, but keep it near enough to the front door to allow you to enter or leave within the time allocated by the entry/exit delay (about 20 seconds). It is a good idea to site the control unit in a cupboard which has a sensor fitted to the door which helps to guard the control unit, although most units have an anti-tamper device fitted which sounds the alarm if anyone tries to tinker with it.

It is a good idea if the control unit has zone control. This allows different areas to be alarmed separately and means, for example, that the upstairs and downstairs can be divided into separate zones, allowing the whole house to be protected while you are out, but allowing the downstairs zone only to be alarmed when you go to bed. Another possibility is to have all the likely entry points, that is exterior doors and windows, wired on one zone, and the other zone can be used to alarm internal doors and pressure mats. This would allow you to activate both zones while you are out of the house, and allow you to switch off the second zone when you are at home so that you can move freely about the house while vulnerable entry points are still guarded.

Ideally the control panel will be mains-powered (connected to the electricity supply through a fused spur) and will have a stand-by battery in case of a power cut.

Detection devices

The control panel is connected to various detection devices. Door and window sensors are the traditional detectors used as perimeter devices – that is, they detect intruders trying to break in. The other types are movement detectors, such as pressure mats and infrared detectors, which are designed to detect intruders who manage to get inside.

Door and window detectors are basically magnetic switches in two parts which are fitted to the opening part of the door or window, and to the fixed frame. If the door or window is kept closed, the magnet keeps the switch contacts inactive, while if the window is opened, the contacts are released and a signal is sent to the control unit which activates the alarm.

There are two basic types of magnetic sensor – open-circuit and closed-circuit. The open-circuit type allows current to flow only when the window is opened; the closed-circuit type allows the current to flow all the time the window is closed: the current only stops when the window is opened. The closed-circuit type is more secure. Both types are also available in surface-mounted and recessed versions. Surface mounted switches are very easy to fit, but do not look neat and are easily tampered with. Recessed switches are invisible when the door or window is closed, being set into recesses in the frame.

Other detectors

Alternatives to magnetic sensors are vibration detectors and breaking-glass detectors. Both types are usually installed by professionals because they need to be carefully set so as to avoid false alarms.

Movement detectors

Important components of a burglar alarm system are movement detectors. The traditional movement detector is the pressure mat. This operates on open-circuit wiring. The mat does not operate while the contacts are open, but pressure on the mat closes the contacts and a signal is sent to the control box.

Sophisticated movement detectors are small wall-mounted units that guard a wide area of a room. If they are strategically placed, only three or four of these movement detectors, together with some door or window contacts, would be sufficient to protect the average house. They need careful setting-up if they are not to create false alarms, so they are usually part of a professionally installed rather than a D-I-Y system.

There are various types of movement detector – the most popular are passive infrared detectors which 'read' the level of infrared radiation in a room. When the pattern changes, when a warm body enters the range of the unit, for example, a signal is sent to activate the control unit. Similar movement detectors are ultrasonic types, and less common are microwave detectors.

Other components

Other components are panic buttons, also called personal alarm switches. These are usually sited by the front door and close to the bed, and are intended for use by the householder to raise the alarm if an intruder is heard at night, or if someone tries to force an entry. Panic buttons are permanently live and can be used at any time.

Component connection

With a good D-I-Y burglar alarm system the components will be con-

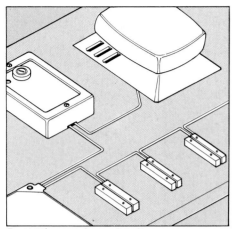

1 With an alarm kit first connect up the components on a bench to understand and test the circuit.

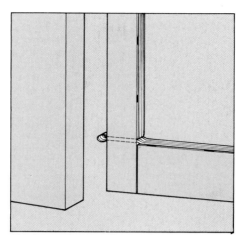

2 A continuous loop circuit connects door and window sensors. Stick cable with pads or hot glue gun.

3 Alternatively, run the cable in mini-trunking, cutting notches at the exit points.

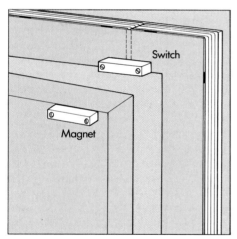

4 A surface sensor is screwed to the fixed frame, and the magnet to the door or window.

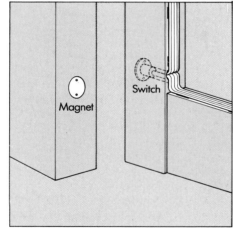

5 If possible, fit recessed sensors and magnets. They are harder to see and tamper with.

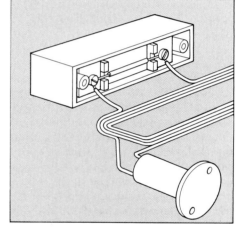

6 Reed switches are connected in series — one wire of the cable is cut and connected to the terminals.

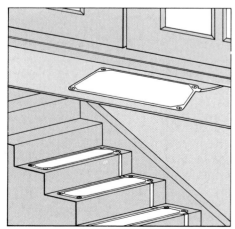

7 Fit pressure pads where an intruder has to move, such as in the hallway, or on consecutive stairs.

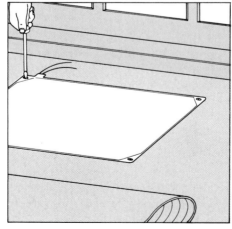

8 Secure pressure pads by screwing through the corner lugs. Only use under fitted carpets.

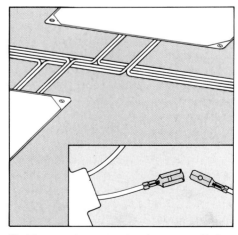

9 The pads are wired in parallel — the two wires are joined to two cables with Lucar connectors (inset).

nected using four-core cable which will allow both closed-circuit devices, such as magnetic contacts, and open-circuit devices, such as pressure mats, to be connected. With the former, the alarm will sound if the cable is cut, but not if the cable is bridged. With open-circuit devices, cutting the connecting wires will not trigger the alarm, but bridging the circuit will.

With four-core cable, one pair of wires is used to form the closed circuit, and one pair for the open circuit. Interfering with the cable will set off one or other of the alarms. For very easy installation, there are also wireless battery-operated remote control alarm systems based on passive infrared detectors with a self-powered siren, flashing strobe light, and magnetic detectors.

Alarm sounders

The two popular types of alarm sounder are bells and sirens. These should be prominently mounted high up on an outside wall so they are difficult to reach but easy to see. The sounder will have integral battery back-up so that it will operate if it is tampered with or if the wires connecting it to the control unit are cut. Some bell covers are designed to be fitted with a flashing light which gives a visual warning that the alarm has been set off, in addition to the sounder. Regulations require that the sound should switch off after about 20 minutes to avoid annoyance to neighbours.

In addition to an external sounder, it is a good idea to have a very loud internal siren as this will help to drive an intruder out of the house as soon as the alarm sounds.

Other devices

If you have a sophisticated alarm installed professionally, it is possible to incorporate devices such as automatic dialling equipment which will make an automatic 999 call and relay a pre-recorded message to the police as soon as the alarm is triggered, or the system may be connected to a digital communicator

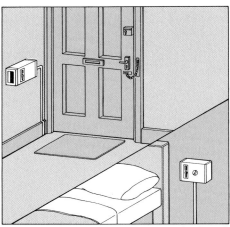

1 Panic buttons are commonly fitted at the hinge side of the front door and by the bedside.

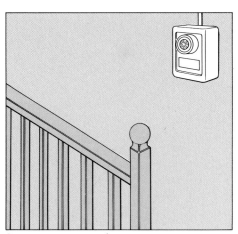

2 Fit an internal siren in a position where it can be heard in all parts of the house.

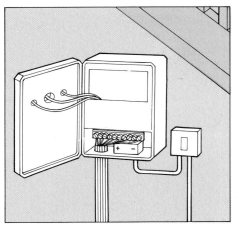

3 A fused connection unit is a good choice of power supply for a rechargeable battery.

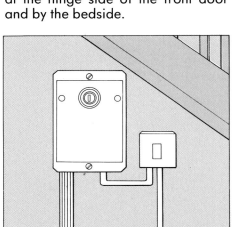

4 When connecting the unit to the alarm circuit cables, keep them separate from any mains cables.

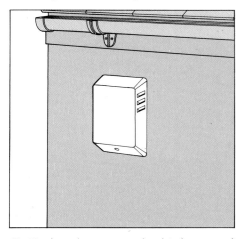

5 Fit the alarm sounder high up and prominently, as an effective, out-of-reach deterrent.

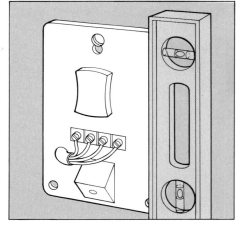

6 Many alarm sounders contain an anti-tamper device and must be fixed perfectly vertical.

Components of a professionally installed system – Telecom Security's 24-hour home-monitoring system. includes the control box, operating keypad, external siren, magnetic door and window contacts, passive infrared sensors, and a smoke detector. The control box contains a remote dialling system which alerts the monitoring station in the event of a break-in or fire.

which can connect the system direct to a central station, usually the alarm company's headquarters. Some systems can distinguish between burglary, personal attack and fire alarms. Systems such as these are ideal for houses in remote areas where there might not be neighbours close enough to respond to an alarm sounder.

Other types of alarms

There are several partial alarm systems that are very easy to install. Mains or battery-operated acoustic alarms looking like hi-fi speakers can be placed unobtrusively on bookshelves and similar places. These detectors react to sharp noises such as breaking glass and sound an integral alarm. Self-contained ultra-

sonic alarms are similar. Also, apart from the passive infrared external light detector units mentioned on page 54, there are portable plug-in systems in which up to ten passive infrared sensors can be connected to a simple plug-in control box. As soon as an intruder is detected, or the system is tampered with, the built-in alarm will sound.

TIMESWITCHES

Automatic time controllers are excellent for reducing the chance of a break-in. Many burglaries take place at night simply because on dark evenings it is much easier for an intruder to check whether a house is occupied simply by looking at the number of lights that are on. By using time switches and various other automatic controls you can make sure that when it gets dark the house looks lived in. A house in darkness with the curtains drawn back is almost inviting attack.

When a light or two is on (not just the porch light and a light in the hall) a potential intruder cannot be certain you are not at home, so he is likely to avoid your house and go on to a house that is definitely unoccupied. Having a radio switched on reinforces the impression that someone is at home.

If you are going out just for an evening, then switching lights on before you go will be as good a way as any of making out that you are at home, as long as the right lights are left on – see pages 54/55. If you have to leave lights on all day with the curtains drawn, because you will be out in the evening or because you are going away for a weekend or longer, simply leaving lights on is not such a good idea.

In these cases you need some form of automatic lighting control. The most popular are automatic timers and the simplest to install and use are plug-in socket timers. They plug into any 13amp socket outlet and control any appliance fitted with a 13amp plug. In practice this usually means a table or standard lamp or a mains-operated radio.

In most cases the timer is programmed to switch on and off at the times you want by pressing small coloured tappets into slots around the edge of a 24-hour timer dial.

Most such timers have a dial marked in 15-minute intervals, and there can be up to five on/off settings per day with the minimum 'on' period being 30 minutes.

1 Passive infrared sensor, control unit and switch; 2 & 3 Photocell- and sound-triggered lamp adaptors;

4 5 & 6 24-hour and 7-day plug-in timeswitches; 7, 8 & 9 Security wall switches replace a lightswitch.

Another type is the electronic digital timer which has a liquid-crystal time-display and up to four on/off settings in a 24-hour period set by pressing setting buttons.

The problem with these timers is that the switching pattern is repeated every day, so if an intruder is watching the house when you are away on a fortnight's holiday, say, he may note the regular pattern and realise that the house is unoccupied.

A way round this one is to use a seven-day timer. In this case the minimum 'on' period may be up to two hours, but the timer can be set to come on and off at different times each day, although the switching pattern will be repeated after a week. Seven-day timers are available in mechanical peg and electronic LCD formats.

A disadvantage with all these timers is that only plug-in lights can be used, which can give away the fact that they are serving as security lighting in an empty house. For this reason it is a good idea to fit either programmable or photoelectric switches in place of conventional light switches.

A programmable switch can switch a room light on and off at preset times which you select, or it can be programmed to memorise the normal switching pattern of the switch and it will repeat this when you are not at home. Photoelectric switches switch on the light as daylight fades and a timer switches off the light at a pre-set time. There are also less sophisticated photoelectric switches for outdoor use which switch exterior lights on at dusk and off at dawn, which is fine for this type of lighting.

Also for outdoor lighting there are proximity detectors, or passive infrared detectors which detect the body heat of anyone approaching the detector (see page 54) and turn on an outside light or lights. Some lights have a built-in passive infrared detector, but more sophisticated sensors can have up to four infrared sensors connected to a controller to switch automatically up to 1100 watts of new or existing outdoor lighting for a period of a few seconds up to four minutes.

Another useful security device is an electric curtain controller which will open and close corded curtain sets, and this can be connected to a timer for automatic control.

4

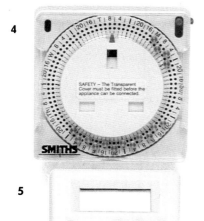

5

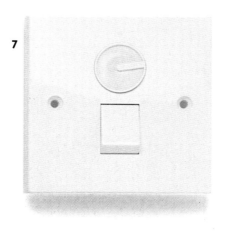

6

7

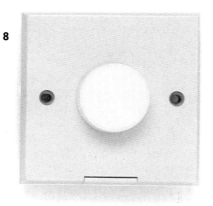

8

9

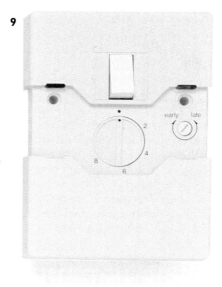

MARKERS, ETC.

There are several ways of improving security in areas not touched on elsewhere. For example, there are various means of marking property, either to prevent it from being stolen in the first place, or to help you to get it back if it is found or recovered by the police.

It is a sad reflection on modern life that with muggings and aggression on the increase there is now a need for personal attack alarms which is not confined solely to women and the elderly, although these groups are more at risk than others.

Even when at home you might not be totally safe, so take sensible precautions when answering the door to callers, or settling down to watch television at night, especially if you are on your own. A viewer and door restraint are musts (see pages 23/25) and when you are at home in the evening and at night it is sensible to bolt the front and back doors to prevent a forced entry. But make sure you can get out quickly if there is a fire.

Security marking

If your property is marked you will have more chance of getting it back if it is lost or stolen. Marking may also act as a deterrent to a burglar because it will make it more difficult to dispose of. However, you do have to think twice about permanently marking antique, silver and gold items, for example, because your marks may drastically reduce their value. Seek professional advice beforehand from your CPO.

Make sure a burglar does not miss your marks by clearly displaying, on doors and windows of your house, notices stating that your property is security marked. Local police and neighbourhood-watch organisers are usually only too willing to supply window stickers to this effect.

The police have established a property-marking code which has become recognised throughout the country. You simply mark your postcode, followed by the number of the house, or the first two or three letters of its name if it does not have a number.

Security marking can either be permanent and visible engraving, or it can be invisible marking which needs a special technique, routinely used on recovered property by the police, to detect. This second method is used by those who feel that visible marking gives a thief the opportunity to remove the marks, while with invisible marking he may miss the marks, allowing police to return the property if and when they recover it. Invisible marking is certainly the best method of marking antiques and other valuable items.

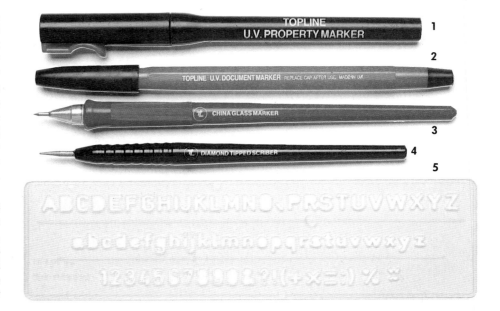

Invisible postcode. . .

. . . appears in UV light.

Above and right:
1 & 2 Broad- and narrow-tipped invisible markers; 3 & 4 Engraving scribers; 5 Letter and number stencil; 6 & 7 Battery and compressed-air personal attack alarms.

Methods of marking include engraving, etching, stamping, indelible marking and invisible marking.

Engraving can be carried out using a small engraving tool of which there are several types, ranging from simple carbide-tipped and diamond-tipped 'pencils' which can be used to scratch a postcode, to small electric-powered engraving tools. To get a neat result, most engravers are supplied with a stencil sheet of letters and numbers.

Etching kits are ideal for marking glass objects, and are widely used for etching the registration number on to car windows. Stencil transfers are used to mask off the security code and acid is brushed on to the surface to etch the code on to the glass.

Sets of number and letter punches are available for die stamping a security mark on to large, heavy metal items, such as bicycle frames and tools. Alternatively, most police stations offer a bicycle frame security stamping service.

Indelible marking is useful on items such as china and ceramic ornaments, and on items made from fabric. An indelible pen is used to put the code permanently on to a concealed surface. A special pen is available for china and ceramics.

Invisible markers are special security pens which allow you to read as you write, but the liquid dries invisible. However, the code shows up when placed under ultraviolet light. Although it is the least damaging method of marking antiques, it is important to take advice before using it on a very valuable item. These marks fade in time,

vidual items of high value, place them against a plain background, get as close as you can, and put a matchbox or other everyday item alongside to give an idea of size. For high value items, it is worth taking views from several different angles, plus close-ups of identifying features, such as hallmarks.

If you have a video camera, a video of the house and its contents, including the contents of cupboards and drawers, could be invaluable if there were ever a break-in or a fire. Be sure to keep negatives or the

alarm if a door is opened. Some are key-operated and some push-button code operated. The better alarms have an entry and exit delay switch which allows you to activate the alarm as you leave the house – a useful adjunct to a conventional burglar alarm system.

There is also a wide range of personal alarms as a deterrent to attacks outdoors. These may be small anti-personnel sirens and whistles working off canisters of compressed air or batteries which emit a painful noise when activated.

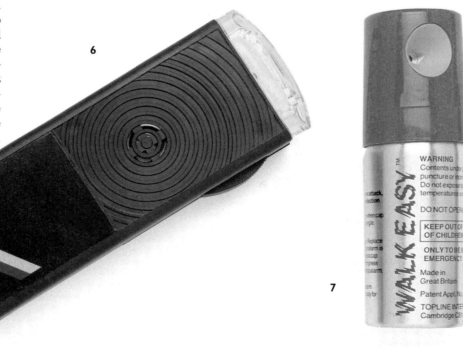

6

7

especially if the item is washed, so buy an ultraviolet light to keep a check on the marks, and renew them from time to time.

Photographing property

Now that indoor photography is so simple, it is well worth photographing everything of a real or sentimental value in case it is ever stolen. It will help you to describe it to the police and insurance company, and could be a great help in getting it back.

If you are photographing indi-

video tapes in a safe place, perhaps in a bank or safe deposit, or at a relative's house, for example.

Personal attack alarms

Many aids to personal security are dealt with on other pages – door chains, and viewers, for example, doorphone intercoms, and panic buttons and personal-attack switches which are often incorporated into burglar alarm systems.

For extra security at night, there are various battery-operated door alarms which sound an instant

to drive off an attacker and attract the attention of passers-by.

Although these devices are small enough to be carried in a pocket or handbag, they are better carried on a neck cord or on the wrist, so that they are instantly ready for use: there would probably not be time to fumble in a handbag in an emergency. If you are in a situation when you consider you are particularly at risk, such as walking home from the station late at night, then carry the device in your hand and be prepared to use it at the first hint of danger.

GARDEN SECURITY

Garden security is a very important aspect of total home security for three reasons. Firstly, by securing the garden itself you make it much harder for an intruder to get to the house, and this could be an important deterrent in itself. Secondly, good security in the garden area, which includes the garage and shed, will ensure that tools, including ladders, which you normally store in these areas cannot be picked up by an intruder and used to break into the house. Finally, there is the importance of securing the equipment that you normally keep in your garden buildings, like lawnmowers and gardening hand tools, and your d-i-y tools. It is easy to forget that the cost of replacing them would run into some hundreds and perhaps even thousands of pounds.

Because of the cheap way many outbuildings are made, before spending a lot of money on expensive locks and other items you must make sure the structure is sound. The best lock in the world will not stop a weak door from being pulled off its hinges, or a few weatherboards from being prised off the side of a shed. Most shed doors open outwards, so it is worth strengthening them, and you should consider fitting hinge bolts, as you would to French windows. If strap hinges are fitted to the door, secure these with at least one coach bolt.

Because of the fact that so many sheds are so easy to break into, consider whether you should store in the shed anything at all that has financial value, or practical value to assist in a break-in.

Shed and garage doors are often flimsy and it is impossible to fit a conventional door lock, even a rim lock. So it is best to use a good padlock with a sturdy locking bar. The locking bar, or hasp, should be made from hardened steel and it should be securely bolted to the door with coach bolts that pass right through the door. These have smooth dome-like heads that are tamper-proof. Do not rely solely on screw fixings for a hasp. Make sure that the locking bar (hasp) is designed to flap over and cover the heads of the fixing bolts and screws, as well as the fixings of the staple (the ring through which the padlock is passed).

The screws for securing hasps and staples should be as long and as thick as possible. The latest type of zinc-plated twin-thread screws are ideal because they are strong, rust-resistant, and threaded up to the screw head which makes them grip firmly. It is important to use zinc-plated screws because rusty screws are weak and eventually pull out very easily.

If the hasp does not flap over the fixing bolts and screw heads, it is a good idea to take steps to ensure that the screws themselves cannot be undone. Screws holding other security fittings and face-fixed strap hinges, for example, can be treated similarly.

With cross-head screws, like Pozidriv, all you have to do is drill out the cross slot after inserting the screw. If you ever need to remove the screw at a later date you will have to drill off the screwhead and refix the fitting slightly to one side.

The alternative is to use clutch-head or non-return screws. These are driven with a conventional flat-blade screwdriver, but the slot is so shaped that the screw can only be inserted and not withdrawn. You can convert ordinary single-slot screws to this type by carefully filing the head as shown in the diagram.

With up-and-over metal garage doors it is usually possible to fit a strong hasp and staple, and a high-quality close-shackle padlock.

With double-leaf wooden garage doors it is common to have a cylinder nightlatch close to the glass panel. This should be changed to a key-operated deadlocking type, or a high quality hasp and staple, and padlock, should be fitted.

Another risk is presented by a garage with a door connecting it to the house. Because the garage can hide an intruder, make sure that this door is very securely barred from inside.

Sometimes garage side-entrance doors, and the doors of outbuildings, are substantial enough for a conventional rim lock to be fitted. Make sure, in this case, that a secure five-lever lock is fitted as well, and not the cheapest and easily picked 'builder's' two-lever type.

Another good way to secure shed doors and side gates is with a pad-bolt. This is like a barrel bolt, but is usually more substantial and galvanised, and has a bolt with a specially shaped handle which can be locked in the closed position with a padlock.

A good padlock should have a case-hardened shackle, a hardened steel body and a mechanism operated by at least five levers or six pins. For highest security choose a close-coupled type; an open shackle could

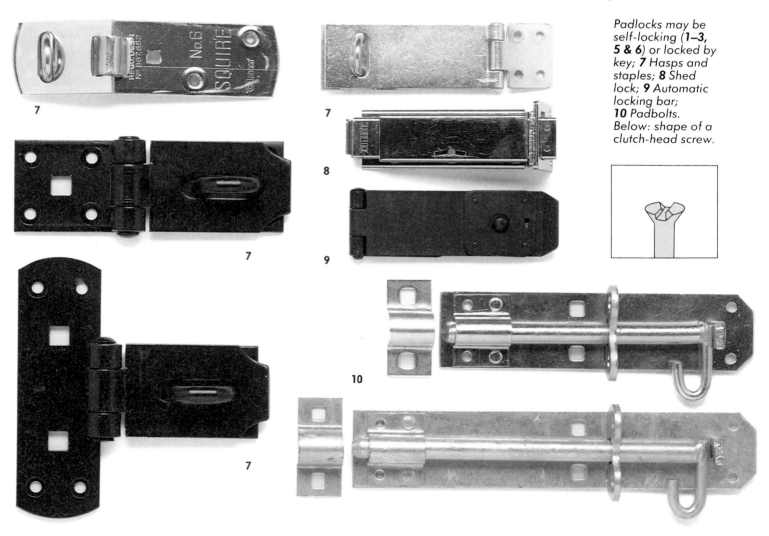

Padlocks may be self-locking (**1–3, 5 & 6**) or locked by key; **7** Hasps and staples; **8** Shed lock; **9** Automatic locking bar; **10** Padbolts. Below: shape of a clutch-head screw.

Right: most of the more commonly used types of boundary fencing are illustrated here. The security rating of each type is indicated in the chart — the more x's, the better the fence is from the security point of view.

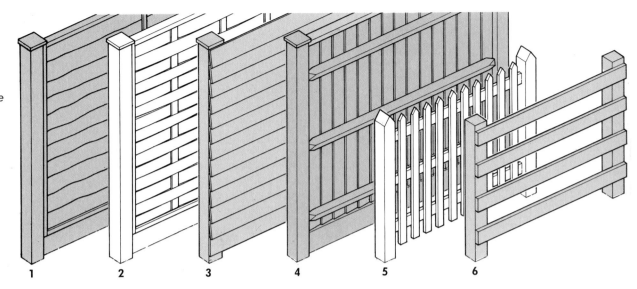

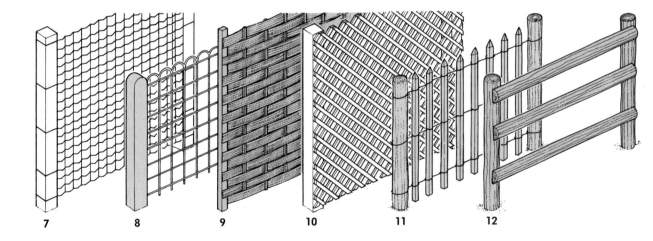

be sawn through or forced open.

Windows can cause problems with sheds, garages and outbuildings generally. They let an intruder see what is inside, which is a bad thing if there are tools visible and other items of value. Fitting obscured glass will prevent this, but it is cheaper to stick self-adhesive frosted glass-effect film over the inside of the windows.

Opening shed and garage windows should be secured with key-operated locks, or simply screw opening frames to the fixed frames if you never open the windows in any case. You can prevent an intruder from breaking a glass pane by re-placing the glass with one of the tough plastic glazing materials that are available.

Some equipment, such as ladders, may be too big to store under cover. In this case it must be properly secured because a ladder is an invaluable tool to an intruder. Sturdy galvanised steel brackets are available which screw to a wall and allow the ladder to be hung horizontally. The brackets are hinged and the top part is designed to link with the lower to which it is secured with a reliable padlock.

The type of garden boundary fence, hedge or wall can have a big effect on the security of a house, especially if it is a house in large grounds, or a property that backs on to an open space, such as a park, fields, or waste ground.

Usually it is best to limit the height of fences or walls at the front of a house so the house (and front door) is in view from the road (and from neighbours' houses opposite). Remember, you need planning permission to put up a fence or wall more than 1m high if it fronts on to a public road, and permission for any fence or wall more than 2m high. Although higher fences and walls are difficult to climb, if they are too high they will prevent neighbourly surveillance even from the upper

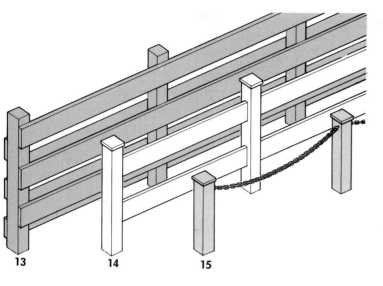

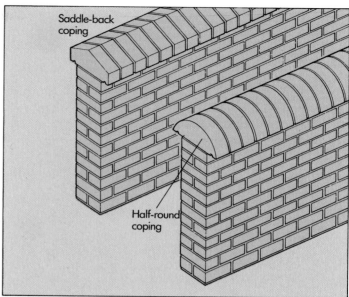

Saddle-back coping

Half-round coping

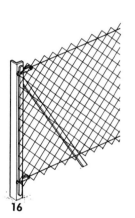

SECURITY RATING

1	Waney-edged overlap panel	xx
2	Interwoven panel	xx
3	Horizontal closeboarded (over 1.5m)	xxx
4	Vertical closeboarded with capping rail (over 1.5m)	xxxxx
5	Picket with pointed palings (over 1.5m)	xxxxx
6	Post and rail	x
7	Welded wire mesh (over 1.5m)	xxxxx
8	Hooped-top wire mesh	xx
9	Woven wattle panel	xx
10	Expandable trellis	xx
11	Split chestnut paling	xxxx
12	Rustic post and rail	x
13	Double ranch	x
14	Ranch	x
15	Post and chain	–
16	Chainlink netting	xxx

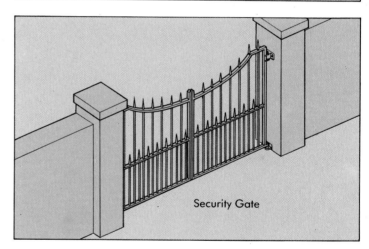

Security Gate

windows of adjacent property and this could allow a criminal to work undisturbed. You need to strike a balance between having a barrier that is difficult to pass through, while at the same time keeping the garden visually acceptable. If nothing else, a fence or wall provides a psychological barrier that may send a burglar off in search of easier pickings. Most intruders like to plan an escape route before they break-in, so where the rear of a house overlooks open land, a high wall or fence can be as useful for hindering a quick escape as it is in preventing unauthorised entry.

Avoid walls with flat tops as these are fairly easy to climb. Coping bricks that form a point or are rounded are harder to climb, especially if the top of the wall is painted with anticlimb paint. This is a thick paint that dries on the outside but remains wet underneath the skin. It is very difficult to grasp and therefore makes fairly high walls hard to climb. It is also useful for painting on to rainwater and plumbing down pipes, but do not use it at heights of less than about 2.2m (7ft) or family and friends may come into contact with it by accident.

Before setting broken glass or barbed wire at the top of a brick wall, check with your local authority in case they have any objections.

When choosing fences for security, avoid those with horizontal rails because they are very easy to climb. Vertical-boarded fences are much better, especially if the boards have pointed tops. You can help to prevent boards from simply being levered out of the way by stapling horizontal wires on the outside of the fence along the fixing points of the boards.

Padlockable gates are valuable in deterring intruders from entering a property, or in the case of a side gate from making a quick getaway from the front garden to the back, or vice versa.

LIGHTING

Lighting improves security in two ways. Personal security and safety are improved because good lighting reduces the risk of accidents such as tripping. Secondly, home security is improved. Intruders prefer to work under cover of darkness, so lighting is a deterrent. Both interior and exterior lighting have valuable benefits for home and personal security. Interior lighting, for example, can give a house the appearance of being occupied when empty; but a house in darkness, on a dark evening, attracts burglars like a magnet. Not only is the house almost certain to be empty if it is not past bedtime, but the cover of darkness allows the thief to break in unhindered. Apart from arranging to leave a light on somewhere, preferably in a bedroom where a burglar cannot peer in on an empty room, it is a good idea to leave a radio on also to suggest even more that the house is occupied.

External lighting is also important because it makes it much harder for a burglar to work unseen.

Internal lighting

To provide automatic control of interior lighting when you are away from home, there is a wide range of timeswitches and photoelectric cells – see pages 46/47. The idea is to give an empty house the appearance of being normally occupied, so avoid the obvious pitfalls, like having only the hall light illuminated or lighting up an uncurtained front room. An easier option is to have the light come on in an upstairs room. Alternatively, you could have partially open venetian blinds in the room with the automatic lighting. It is very difficult to see through these to tell if the room is occupied or not. Partially closed blinds do not look out of place during the day, and because it makes a lot of noise to break through venetian blinds burglars rarely attempt to break into such rooms.

External lighting

Apart from deterring a potential thief, outdoor lighting has other useful benefits. It welcomes guests to your home and you do not have to fumble for your key on a dark night. It can also be reassuring to be able to see that there is no one lurking near the front door.

Although the object of the garden lighting may be to improve security, there is no need for the fittings to be purely functional. Mains or low-voltage decorative garden lighting sets may not be as bright as plain halogen floodlights, but carefully placed coloured lights can be as big a deterrent to a burglar as a 300 watt floodlight.

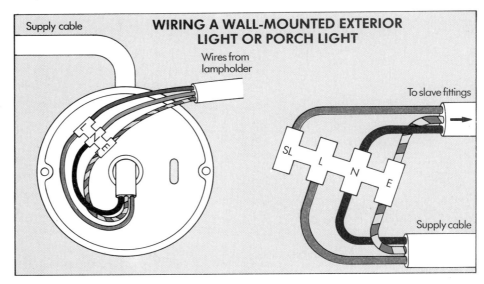

WIRING A WALL-MOUNTED EXTERIOR LIGHT OR PORCH LIGHT

Supply cable

Wires from lampholder

To slave fittings

Supply cable

Connect the supply cable into the terminals on the light fitting, as instructed. Pass the cable through the wall in plastic conduit angled down towards the outside.

Fittings with a built-in PIR sensor may have a slave facility for operating extra lights.

There is a very wide range of outdoor light fittings from which to choose, including bulkhead and globe fittings for mounting on walls above or adjacent to doorways, lights and lanterns on brackets for wall-mounting, pendant lanterns and ceiling-mounted light fittings for porches, modern and traditional-style post-mounted fittings for illuminating paths, drives, steps and slopes, and ground-spike mounted spotlights and floodlights for general garden and tree and shrub illumination.

As already mentioned, timers and photoelectric cells can be used to turn exterior lights on at preset times, or when it gets dark – see pages 46/47 – but another excellent security fitting is the passive infra-red (PIR) sensor. This type of sensor detects body heat, and senses the approach of a person, turning on the light automatically. Few intruders will linger if suddenly bathed in light, and it can be useful to be welcomed by a light while you look for your key. Many light fittings have a built-in PIR sensor.

When siting outdoor lights remember that the object is to ensure that there are as few shadows as possible. By careful positioning of a few light fittings it should be possible to arrange to have a wide spread of light. Obviously a light over or beside front and back doors is essential. A bright floodlight fixed high up and out of reach above a door is an excellent way of illuminating a

1 & 2 Wall- and spike-mounted low-voltage garden spotlights; *3* Bulkhead lights with integral PIR sensor; *4* Twin spotlight with integral PIR sensor; *5* Single globe wall-light; *6* Security wall-lantern with PIR sensor. Fittings including those with an integral PIR sensor, may have a photocell to prevent daytime operation.

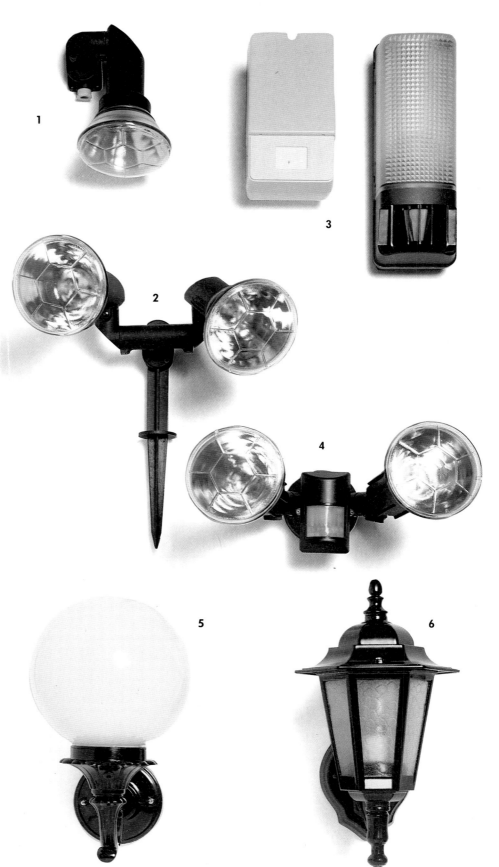

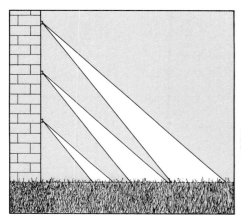

The height and angle of a PIR sensor affect its range and the area of ground covered by the beam.

large area. Lights fixed to brackets at the corner of a house have the benefit of throwing light along two walls at once. Make sure the lights do not annoy neighbours – they are your best allies against crime!

Because an enclosed porch is secluded, this is frequently used by intruders when attempting to break in, so good lights here are a strong deterrent. Either a wall-mounted or a ceiling fitting can be chosen.

All lights attached to the outside of a house must be waterproof. They can be connected to one of the household lighting circuits using a junction box with a separate cable going to a switch (waterproof if positioned outside), or to the ring circuit by means of a switched fused connection unit. The cable to the light can be run through the wall of the house, with all the wiring done from inside. Angle the hole slightly downwards to the outside and seal with mastic.

SAFES

If you have small valuable items you cannot afford to lose, such as jewellery, small items of sentimental value, and important documents, like the deeds to your property, your will, insurance policies, or passports, then it is a good idea to protect them in a safe. You can either buy and install your own safe, or you can use a commercial safe or vault.

Using a commercial safe is a popular choice for items of considerable value. It probably costs more than buying your own safe, but the items stored should be more secure. Against the cost of storage, you may make a saving due to lower household insurance premiums.

If you choose to buy your own safe, then it should be hidden away in the hope that an intruder will not find it. Never tell anyone that you have a safe, and hope that if an intruder does find it he will not waste time trying to open it. Remember also, if it is documents and files that you need to keep, that not all safes give protection against fire.

Using a commercial safe deposit

A popular choice is to deposit valuables at a bank. Most banks have this facility for which they usually make a charge. The actual amount will depend on the size of the package or deed box which you want stored, and how often you need access to it.

Usually, it is best to use facilities of this type for documents, such as property deeds, which you will rarely need to see. For items which may be needed more frequently, such as jewellery, it may be better to use a safety deposit box.

Safety deposit boxes are strong locked boxes kept in securely guarded underground vaults. They are available in larger towns and cities, and may be operated by the high street banks or private security companies. You have your own locked box and only you know what is in it. You pay for the size of safety deposit box you hire, and for each visit. Unlike depositing valuables in a bank, where access is restricted to banking hours, access to safety deposit boxes is usually over a much longer period, and at weekends, so these are more useful for items such as jewellery which may be required in the evening.

Home safes

Domestic safes are really the last line of defence in the battle against burglary. If it is well hidden, an inexpensive domestic safe will give reasonable security for valuables and important documents.

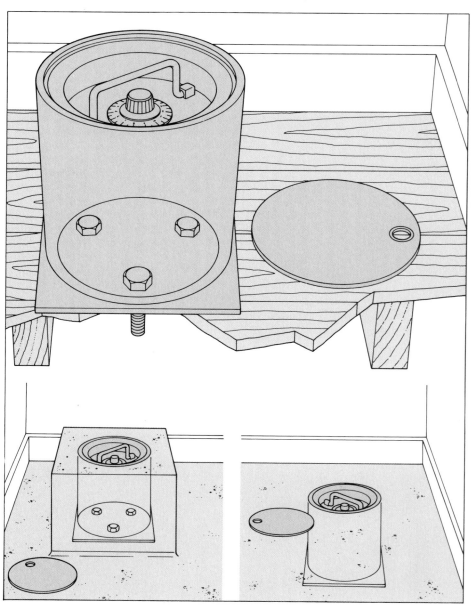

Above: This safe is suitable for surface or flush mounting on wood or concrete floors.

Above right: For flush fitting under a timber floor, a surrounding framework of joists is built.

Floor safes

Floor safes are probably the best type of domestic safe. They can easily be hidden under a carpet or other floor covering and they offer a high degree of security.

The best type of under-floor safe is made of thick steel with a small but strong lid and is set into a reinforced concrete floor.

Ideally, this type of safe is installed when you are having the house built, but if you have a house with solid floors, then this type can still be fitted. The work will entail making a hole in the concrete, which will mean hiring an electric breaker hammer from a tool hire shop. Make the hole considerably larger than the safe, if possible in a corner of the room to give a burglar less room to work if he does discover the safe.

You can site the safe in any room, but avoid a room where the floor is likely to get wet, such as a laundry room or bathroom. The usual hiding place for a floor safe is under a carpet square or rug, and this may be the first place an intruder would look, but do not neglect other, less obvious places. Even in a room like a kitchen with a tiled floor it may be possible to hide a safe under a false floor in the base of a cupboard.

Making a large hole for the safe will ensure that the safe is well embedded in concrete. The work will definitely involve breaking through the damp-proof membrane in the floor, and this should be made good by lining the hole with heavy-duty polythene. Reinforce the concrete around the safe with concrete reinforcing mesh or rods.

Under-floor safes can be fitted in suspended timber floors, but these do not offer the security of safes set in concrete. These safes are secure boxes, often with combination locks, which fit between adjacent joists and bolt or screw to them. Choose a position which is reasonably accessible without being an obvious hiding place. Prepare the opening by fitting two short trimmer joists between the joists exposed after lifting the floorboards, and if necessary fit another joist between the trimmers to create an opening into which the floor safe will fit snugly. The safe is then fitted

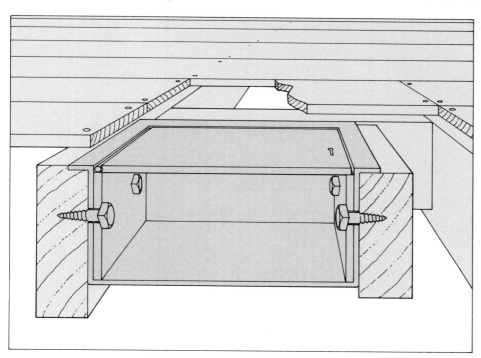

FITTING A FLOOR SAFE IN A TIMBER FLOOR

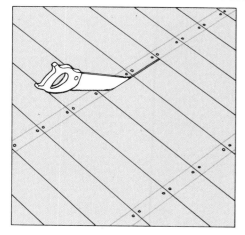

1 Cut away the floorboards to the required aperture, using a circular saw or a floorboard saw.

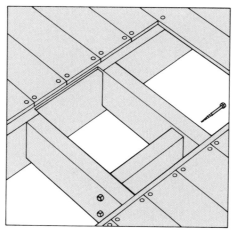

2 Make a sturdy, close-fitting support for the safe by fitting trimmer joists glued and screwed in place.

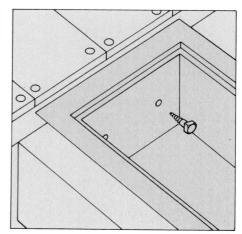

3 Screw the safe in position from inside. The lid of the safe closes over the fixing screws to protect them.

by bolting or screwing to the joists from the inside following the manufacturer's instructions. The floorboards are replaced, cutting them as necessary to fit around the safe. Finally, the safe is covered with a sheet of plywood or hardboard to bring the surface level with the surrounding floorboards.

Wall safes

Wall safes are small security boxes that are built into a wall, replacing one or more bricks. The classic place for hiding a wall safe is behind a picture, and this is where a burglar will look first. So think carefully about concealing a wall safe – its main security value lies in not being discovered because while a wall safe is quite easy to build into a masonry wall, it is also quite easy to knock out, especially in an older house where the mortar is crumbly. A burglar will know this, and if he finds a wall safe while you are not at home, he may well be prepared to risk making a noise in order to remove the safe which he can work on later.

At least one manufacturer has got round the problem by disguising his wall safe as an electrical power point. Good hiding places for conventional wall safes are in rooms where wall safes are not expected.

When choosing a wall safe, buy the largest size that is practical. Some will fit in a single thickness of brick wall, which is useful if you have cavity walls. Others are deeper for fixing into 230mm (9in) thick, or deeper, solid brick walls.

Fixing is a matter of chopping out bricks to take the wall safe and re-building the wall with strong bricks or masonry and cement mortar. Most types have fixing lugs, flanges, bolts or screws that go into the mortar surrounding the safe. If it is necessary to make fixings into the surrounding wall, make sure that the brickwork is strong enough to take this.

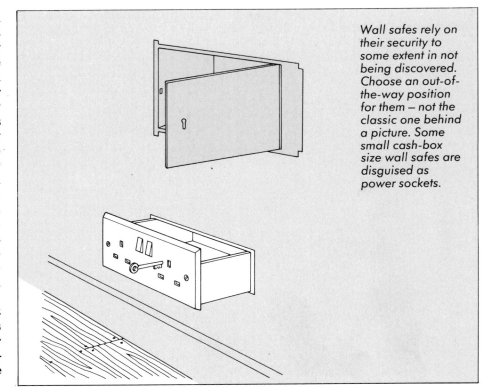

Wall safes rely on their security to some extent in not being discovered. Choose an out-of-the-way position for them – not the classic one behind a picture. Some small cash-box size wall safes are disguised as power sockets.

FITTING A WALL SAFE

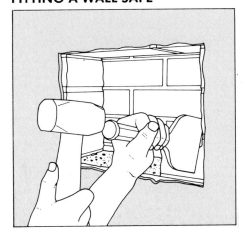

1 Select a suitable position for the safe and with a bolster chisel, chop out bricks as specified.

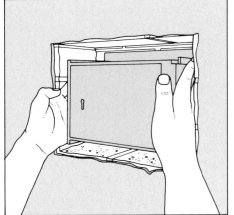

2 Position the safe flush with the wall and temporarily hold it with packing pieces or wall fixings.

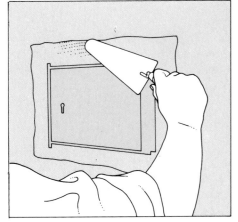

3 Use a fine concrete mix to set the safe in place. Later make good around the safe using finish plaster.

SAFETY

It is often said that accidents do not just happen – they are caused. In the home thousands of injuries are sustained each year by young and old alike. Tragically, some injuries prove to be fatal.

This section of the book concentrates on potentially dangerous aspects and activities in and around the home and garden. It highlights many common errors and tells you how to avoid them. It is up to each one of us to get into good habits, to do things properly, never to take a chance where there is potential danger and to make sure children are protected by alerting them to the importance of always placing safety first. It is only by pursuing good standards with commonsense and always being vigilant that we can prevent ourselves and our families from becoming accident statistics. Learn to take as much care over the small jobs as over the major ones.

GENERAL ADVICE

Every day many hundreds of people are injured, some fatally, due to accidents in the home. Cuts, broken limbs, burns, poisoning and electric shocks are all happening every hour. The numbers can be drastically reduced simply by being careful.

Take a look around your own home and, using these pages as a reference, look at it in a completely new light. You may be surprised at the dangers lurking there. Very often an obvious hazard will have been there for some years; it will have become something the whole family has learned to live with. When the inevitable happens and someone gets hurt you will be telling yourself that you should have done something about it years ago!

Start at your garden gate. Walk up the path. Is it crumbling in places? Is there a loose slab or pothole to trip someone up? Immediately you may start finding faults.

The entrance should be well lit with a bright porch light since usually there are a couple of steps.

Now open the front door and have a look at that mat inside. If it is badly positioned or there is a parquet floor or vinyl below then someone could trip over it or slide on it. The answer is to make a recess for it in the floor.

Inspect the stairs. Make sure that the treads are in good repair; see that the banister rail is safe and that any spindles are sound. A missing one could leave a gap wide enough for a child to squeeze through. Make sure that the carpet is anchored firmly and not badly worn. Check that the lighting is bright enough.

In living rooms think about floor-coverings – are they loose in the doorway, rucked up or slippery? If you have rugs make sure they are fixed at the edges. Wooden floors can be dangerous if highly polished.

Consider the arrangement of the furniture in the rooms. Are some dangerously positioned so that someone could collide with a sharp edge? A simple rearrangement could save bumps and bruises.

There should be a guard in front of the fire or room heater and, if you do have an open fire or heating appliance in the fireplace, do not have a mirror above it – there is a risk of burns while attention is distracted.

Trailing flexes are a hazard so check lamps, televisions, stereo and so on. Either find new positions for the appliances or perhaps install extra strategically placed sockets.

Trailing flex

Mirror over fireplace

Unguarded fire

Loose scatter rug

Slippery floor

Badly placed furniture

Poor lighting

Loose paving slabs

Door mat to trip the unwary

Unlit steps

Pot holes

Kitchen

Danger lurks everywhere in the kitchen. A well planned kitchen will minimise risks but there may well be room for improvement.

Potentially, the most dangerous kitchen layout is the one with a door at both ends – one leading to the garden. This becomes a 'main highway' for all the family to go through which can be an enormous risk when a meal is being prepared. One thing you must ensure is that the working area is situated along one wall with cooker and sink close together or with a continuous work surface between. Avoid at all costs having the cooker and sink opposite each other.

This entails carrying red-hot cookware across the corridor – perhaps with children running through.

On this aspect it is a good idea to have a safety guard for saucepans fitted to the cooker.

There is plenty of 'trouble' lurking behind cupboard doors and drawers in the form of bleach, sharp knives and suchlike so make sure these are inaccessible to little fingers. Fit childproof locks if necessary.

Bedrooms

Bedrooms are normally safe places, bearing in mind again the condition of floor-coverings and positioning of furniture. In a child's room you may need to fit vertical window bars or a secure lock to prevent a toddler from climbing on to the sill and falling through the window. Either arrangement allows you to ventilate the room without risk. A lock that allows a window to be secured in a slightly open position is easy to fit.

Do not put things on shelves which a child may attempt to reach by climbing on a dangerous 'hop-up'. Check for sharp corners and edges – round them off if necessary.

Make sure that a cot is coated with lead-free paint since toddlers do love to chew. Painted toys similarly need lead-free paint.

Bathrooms

There must not be a power point in the bathroom.

If you have a vinyl or cork floor make sure you have a non-slip rug. Floors can be slippery when wet.

Garden

Finally, check the garden. Make sure that any fish pond, however shallow, is covered where there are children. Never leave tools and equipment lying around.

Outbuildings, sheds and garages are irresistible playrooms and hiding places for small children. In them can often be found an armoury of dangerous tools and chemicals. So make sure they are kept locked whenever there is not a responsible adult around to keep an eye.

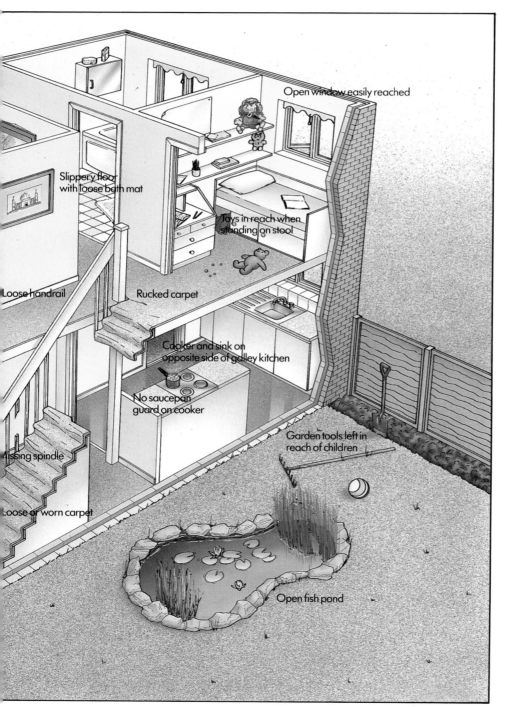

Open window easily reached

Slippery floor with loose bath mat

Toys in reach when standing on stool

Loose handrail

Rucked carpet

Cooker and sink on opposite side of galley kitchen

No saucepan guard on cooker

Garden tools left in reach of children

Missing spindle

Loose or worn carpet

Open fish pond

SAFETY CLOTHING

In industry, people are now well used to wearing safety clothing to protect themselves from being hurt by materials or machinery. The rules and regulations are there to ensure that they can work comfortably and confidently irrespective of the job they are doing or what they are handling.

The rules have been in force for many years and now it comes as a natural habit to put on a safety helmet, protective gloves, goggles and so on. It was not always the case – it was almost considered a chore to put something on before starting work but now everyone has come to realize the value of safety clothing. It is something that, happily, is beginning to spill over into domestic situations.

There are many jobs which home-owners, and DIY enthusiasts especially, have to tackle which are dirty, potentially dangerous, or just unpleasant.

In almost every job there is a possibility of the person harming themselves in some way – and not always through carelessness. Even the most organised, efficient worker can be prone to an accident.

Danger comes in many guises and they are not always obvious. A spinning circular saw, a blowtorch, a high ladder present obvious hazards but the fumes from a tin of adhesive or the fine dust thrown up when sanding down paintwork are often not connected with risky activity. Wearing safety clothes should come as automatically as putting on specialized everyday clothing when the occasion warrants it. After all, you would not got out into a rainstorm without putting on a raincoat or taking an umbrella; and few would step out into deep snow without wearing wellington boots.

As with basic home security, where you must remember to lock windows and doors, safety clothes precautions start with simple commonsense. Loose clothes, scarves, necklaces, ties, can all get caught in moving parts of machinery. So roll up your sleeves or make sure your sleeves are buttoned if necessary. If you have long hair, tie it back.

Make sure your footwear is matched to the job – for normal d-i-y tasks this will simply mean putting on strong shoes when working from a ladder, for example. If you stand on rungs for a long time wearing only trainers or plimsoles your feet will soon let you know.

If you have to mend a leaking roof or gutter when it is pouring down then put on waterproof clothing. If it is cold, put on a warm sweater, coat and gloves as necessary. If you are not used to physical activity, remember that digging quickly in the garden or clearing snow vigorously can cause heart problems for certain people. The sun can be harmful too so think about a sunhat, neck and shoulder protection and so on: use a sun cream and avoid lengthy exposure.

A complete safety outfit.

Gloves

Protective gloves are available in various materials which will avoid damage to your hands when working with dangerous tools, materials or corrosive liquids. Heavy-duty industrial gloves in leather give the best protection since they have features such as reinforced palms, fingertips and knuckles.

Lighter PVC gloves are also excellent when working with oils, greases and most chemicals.

Natural rubber gloves are stronger than the 'washing-up' quality found in most homes. They withstand chemicals and have excellent resistance to tears and abrasions which can cause dangerous leaks.

Knitted gloves with the palm and back reinforced with latex are excellent for carrying glass and metal since they are non-slip.

Metalworkers, car enthusiasts and so on will know that for using welding equipment heavy duty welding gauntlets are a must.

Keen gardeners will automatically don a sensible pair of gardening gloves when setting off with the pruners to tackle a rose bush or other prickly job.

Dust masks and respirators

The list of jobs which create airborne particles and fumes is almost endless. Inhaling these can have both short- and long-term effects so it is clearly desirable to slip on a face mask before starting work. It is sometimes thought that you only need to wear a mask when working indoors in a confined space where dust is contained. This may be the worst kind of working condition but even outdoors you need protection.

The simplest face mask consists of

an aluminium-framed filter holder which moulds easily to the shape of your face. This is used with a replaceable cotton gauze pad that covers the nose and mouth. This is ideal for lighter dust situations – sanding wood, plaster etc.

Cup masks give relief from coarse, non-toxic and nuisance dusts – so put one on when working conditions are a little more rigorous. Cup masks are disposable.

Respirators are more robust being made from moulded rubber or plastic. They have an exhalation valve and a replaceable cartridge filter.

The filter resists organic vapour and paint spraying. You have to use the appropriate filter for the substance being used.

Safety glasses

A flying particle of rust or paint is like a piece of glass or a nail. The

Dust and splash protection:
1 Lightweight and heavy-duty overalls; **2** Safety goggles; **3** Safety specs; **4** Cotton pad dust-mask; **5** Respirator.

damage it can do to an eye is severe. Simple dust or grit floating in the air can also be painful and irritating if it gets into your eyes. The same can be said for liquids.

Some typical jobs requiring eye protection would be, for example, painting a ceiling with textured compound, spraying ordinary paint or using creosote or preservative to treat fences, sheds and so on. Into this category comes spraying insecticides – as gardeners will testify, a sudden breeze in the wrong direction can be irritating in more ways than one, and possibly dangerous.

Many metalwork jobs – grinding and drilling for example – cause metal swarf to fly through the air, as does cutting stone and brick.

Whenever you are using toxic chemicals – and especially when working overhead, make eye-protection your priority. Paint stripping with chemicals is a case in point; no matter how careful you are in brushing on a chemical, gravity takes over and the chemical may drip down from a banister rail or spindle just above eye level. Obviously the best course is always to be looking down on the work area when using chemicals but this is not always possible to organize.

In their simplest form, safety glasses are like ordinary spectacles but with impact resistant lenses; some are held in place with an elastic grip. More sophisticated versions have features such as ventilated side protection and non-fogging lenses. Many types can be worn over ordinary spectacles. Recognising the natural resistance, especially of the young, to wearing safety specs, manufacturers have produced designer frames in a range of colours.

Safety goggles are most robust with safety lenses housed in a flexible PVC frame. They have an adjustable elastic headband. Gas welding goggles have a shaded lens. Most types can be worn over spectacles.

Ear protectors

Prolonged exposure to noise can cause damage to the ears, headaches and even mental disturbance. Oddly, though, some people adapt quite quickly to the loudest piece of machinery to the point where they are not affected by it at the time. It is only when they switch off that they remember the decibels that have been pumping out.

Foam earplugs with a connecting cord for easy removal are available. These can give protection to noise levels in excess of 80 decibels. Ear capsules or muffs are usually mounted on an adjustable headband and have interchangeable ear pads.

One of the big problems with some earplugs is that they also prevent the user from hearing a warning shout should an emergency develop – such as a falling tree branch, roof tile or whatever. For this reason check if the protectors you are buying allow you some awareness of sound so that you can react at a dangerous moment.

Safety helmets

The industrial yellow 'hard hat' is familar to us on all building sites. They are constructed of high density polythene or glass fibre and have a fully adjustable internal polythene harness for comfort and fit.

A helmet protects you against falling masonry or will cushion the impact should you be unlucky enough to fall from scaffolding or a ladder.

Generally speaking, though, a safety helmet would only be needed for the d-i-yer who is going to undertake a sizeable demolition or building project. For smaller 'building site' jobs many people will prefer to hire a helmet for a day or two.

Safety boots

Anyone who has ever dropped a brick or paving slab on their foot will be the first to vouch for the commonsense thinking behind wearing safety boots when building walls, laying a path or other similar heavy building work.

Good work boots have features such as steel-reinforced toe caps, hardwearing leather uppers and oil-resistant rubber soles.

With footwear, it is a matter of horses for courses. Safety boots are the first choice for building work but not for keeping out wet and muddy water. So for 'trench warfare' buy strong rubber wellingtons.

Knee pads

Gardeners know all about the necessity for knee pads! Hours of kneeling down weeding flower beds can cause massive discomfort without protection. Do-it-yourselfers are less familiar with them and find themselves either having to stop continuously to straighten up and ease those aching joints, or having to stoop in an awkward position when laying floor tiles, painting skirtings and other low-level jobs. Knee protection also prevents injuries such as splinters picked up from rough wood surfaces – joists, for example – and abrasions from stony ground or gravel.

Lightweight polyurethane foam knee pads have an elasticated strap – they are ideal for most around-the-house-and-garden jobs. Heavy duty expanded synthetic rubber moulded pads have adjustable rubber straps. These can be worn for longer jobs especially those where the user has to kneel on an abrasive surface.

Protective overalls

Most people have an outfit of old working clothes which is brought out when there is a dusty or dirty job to be done. They only tend to get too bad to wear after they have become splattered with paint, oil or a chemical. You may even be one of those people who do not tackle too many jobs and have no really old clothes to wear. In either case the answer is a pair of overalls which you can slip over your clothes to protect them from paint, chemicals and water splashes.

Lightweight polypropylene suits are ideal since they do not weigh you down when you are working. They are highly rip-resistant and better styles feature such things as elasticated sleeve cuffs and deep pockets in which tools and materials can be stored.

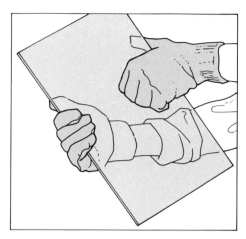

Wear heavy-duty gloves to handle glass for good grip and to prevent cuts. PVC gloves give protection against chemicals and greases.

Ear defenders make noisy tools more comfortable to handle: make sure you can still hear warning noises.

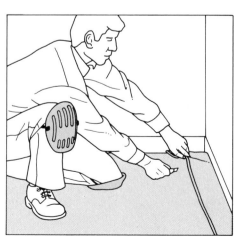

Knee pads prevent aching joints in jobs where you cannot stand or sit. They also prevent abrasion.

You can keep a set of lightweight overalls in the car boot so that you can slip them on at any time to protect your clothes when an emergency arises and a wheel has to be changed or a fan belt replaced.

Chainsaw kit

The chainsaw has become very popular with do-it-yourselfers in the past few years – especially those people who make regular trips to cut logs for fires and stoves. The speed at which a long, heavy branch can be reduced to small logs demonstrates its awesome power.

If you ever use or hire a chainsaw then get the right safety gear to go with it. If you own your own chainsaw and use it regularly then consider investing in a complete safety kit.

As least one company manufactures a complete kit which comes in a holdall to stop items 'straying'.

The kit comprises a safety helmet complete with visor and ear defenders. Chrome leather safety gloves and protective gaiters are included – the latter to stop ankle injuries. They should be used in conjunction with steel toe-capped safety boots which have to be bought separately.

Finally, and very important, there are safety leggings. These comprise several layers of loose polyester fibres sandwiched between the water resistant nylon outer fabric and the cotton lining. In the unlikely event of their coming into contact with the moving chain they will cause it to stop the saw in a fraction of a second.

Once you have bought some safety clothes, get into the habit of using them whenever required. It takes only a few seconds to slip on some gloves or goggles – keep your gear near your tool kit so that you reach for both at the same time. Nothing is worse than having spent money on an item and then forgetting to wear it and injuring yourself.

Finally, remember, safety clothes are a last means of protection. They do not leave the way clear for you to be careless in the way you handle tools and materials.

AVOIDING INJURIES

Most injuries in and around the home can be avoided simply by commonsense. Unfortunately, most people learn only through breaking the rules and suffering for it afterwards.

Accidents do not just happen – they are caused. Laziness, forgetfulness, eagerness to finish quickly, untidyness – these are the root causes of many an injury. Here we concentrate on some of the things which should become automatic habits to do, or avoid. In other chapters you can find out about the correct use of tools, chemicals, ladders and so on, plus protective safety clothes.

Back problems account for more absenteeism from work than anything else. Everyone of us knows someone who is frequently unable to get to work because their back has 'gone again'. There are many reasons why some people develop problems – poor posture and being generally unfit contribute but a good many can be put down to having tackled a DIY project without taking due care.

A good many people, office workers and others who are not required to put great physical effort into their daily lives, and perhaps who do not take physical exercise, are in the high risk category.

Simply because they are not used to it, their body cannot cope with the strenuous demands imposed on it by a hard day's DIY. Even a 'lightweight' task such as wallpapering or painting a ceiling can be very tiring but it is nothing to the toll that a few hours concreting or digging foundations can take.

So the first thing to remember is that heavy work should be undertaken in shifts of only a couple of hours. When planning ahead you may think this will make the job last for ever but rushing at it can even-

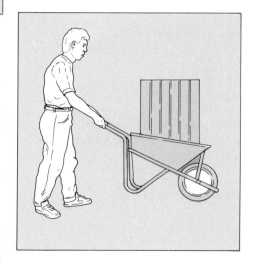

Always keep your back straight when lifting

tually cause even greater delays through an injury.

Many hands make light work so try and get a helper or two along to make things easier. If you are having a load of ready-mix concrete delivered, then you can take turns in trundling the wheelbarrow from the lorry to your building site.

There are many things around the house which you might want to replace or take out and which, if you are not prepared, can turn out to be extremely heavy – far more so than you ever imagined.

A tiled fireplace surround is a fine example. Behind the tiles there may be a ton weight of a reinforced concrete shell. Once you have cut through the bolts holding it to the wall it could topple forward and cause a broken foot if you do not leap out of the way in time.

A cast iron bath is another case in point. You might be able to drag it to the top of the stairs – but try and lower it down single-handed.

Use a wheelbarrow or trolley to move heavy weights

In both cases – fireplaces and bath – the answer to getting them out of the house is to cover them in an old thick sheet or blanket and then break them into smaller, manageable pieces with a sledge hammer. The cover will stop pieces from flying around causing damage to you or to your room. Even so, be sure to wear safety goggles, just in case of stray fragments.

Attempting to lift heavy objects is a major cause of back problems, and can also cause aches and pains in knees and other joints. The classic

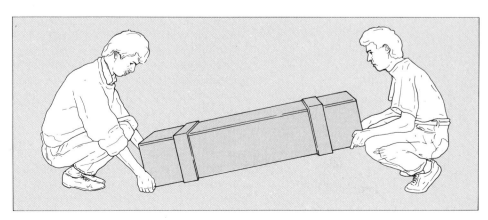

An extra pair of hands is invaluable where heavy work is concerned

case is a bag of cement; this is also an awkward shape to get a secure hold on. Very often at the builder's merchant, one of the people working in the yard will put a bag in the boot of your car for you. It is when you get home that problems start. You are standing in a hopeless position for lifting a heavy weight and both your back and arms will be stretched to the limit. The same applies if you have to lift a bag of cement, heavy stone or paving slab off the ground.

The golden rule when lifting is to keep your back straight. So, squat down – do not bend – grasp the object close to your chest and stand up straight. Note the importance of grasping the object close to you – never extend your arms.

If you cannot lift something comfortably and correctly then get help.

Too many hours

Always plan a sensible working day. Start early, have a mid-morning and mid-afternoon break and a proper lunch. Do not work on to the small hours. When you work too long, you can get sloppy. Discipline evaporates and work standards deteriorate. What is worse, you start to take chances.

Danger points

Potentially the most dangerous place in the house is the stairs. A sensible DIY job is to check regularly that the staircarpet is well anchored. This is vital where where are older people or children – although even the most sure-footed and agile can easily come to grief. If there is not a good handrail on the stairwell wall, fit one; it is a simple DIY job. So, too, is making a safety gate to keep youngsters away from harm. Basic commonsense is to make sure toys, bags and so on are never left on the stairs. Check that lighting is adequate (do not delay in changing a dead bulb) and that you can switch on and off from upstairs and downstairs.

Do inspect doorways where floorcoverings get most wear and are likely to turn up. It does not take

long to fit binder bars to secure any kind of floorcovering.

Slippery floors are very dangerous. When you mop the floor keep people away until it is dry.

Do remember when you are in the loft that you must stand only on the joists. Between them – probably hidden below insulation – is the thin ceiling of the room below. If you stand on that you will probably put your foot right through it.

Safety gate

A staircase safety gate is a simple woodwork project yet it is vital in every home once a baby starts to crawl. The design here can be altered to suit the opening width of the staircase. In some cases a gate at both the top and bottom of the stairs could be needed.

Some general design points are:
1 All wood should be well sanded to remove splinters.
2 A reasonable minimum height would be 750mm (30in) though 900mm (3ft) is needed as a toddler grows.
3 The design must not incorporate any horizontal footholds which would enable the child to climb.

4 The spacings between the vertical side frames and all spindles, and the base of the gate and the floor should be between 60 and 90mm (2½ and 3½in).

The wall posts and gate frame can be made from 75 × 50mm (3 × 2in) softwood and the spindles should be 19mm (¾in) diameter dowel.

Fix one wall post securely to the wall on one side using No. 10 screws. Screw the other wall post direct to the existing newel post on the other side of the staircase.

Drill matching dowel holes for the spindles in the top and bottom frame members. Remember, when cutting the spindles, to allow for 25mm (1in) at each end to enter the frame members.

Join the vertical side members to the top and bottom members using dowels and glue. Allow time for the glue to set before hanging the gate using two butt hinges, and fixing furniture bolts, top and bottom, on the locking side.

The gate must not open on to the stairs: it must pull back on to the landing.

If necessary, more secure locking bolts can be fitted.

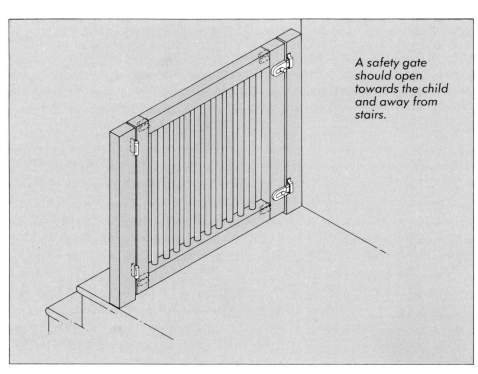

A safety gate should open towards the child and away from stairs.

ADHESIVES AND CHEMICALS

The greatest danger of adhesives and other chemicals found in every house in the country is that they are not always seen as a danger. Everyone recognises the fact that climbing a ladder or scaffold contains an element of risk; it is easy to look at a circular saw slicing through a thick piece of wood and imagining what it could do to your fingers; and a blowtorch or hot-air gun can clearly cause burns.

However, we are so used to having adhesives, cleaners and other bottles, tubes and tins around us that it is easy to forget just how dangerous these things can be: modern products are extremely efficient and powerful. Only if properly stored and used can they do their job in total safety.

So obey the rules and never underestimate the power of a chemical or adhesive. Most important of all, keep children away from these bright and appealing tins and tubes. Little minds cannot be expected to understand that colourful containers do not all contain sweets and chocolates.

When 'glue-sniffing' among certain unfortunate young people came into the news it was probably the first time that many people came to realise that a tin or tube of adhesive was anything more than a normal household product. It was probably kept alongside the washing-up liquid in a kitchen cupboard and regarded in exactly the same vein.

The only other publicity that the danger of adhesives really receives is through the 'super-glues' when through accident or deliberate action an unfortunate victim is injured and has to visit the casualty department of a local hospital for emergency treatment on hands, mouth, eyes or whatever.

You have obviously noticed the pungent odour that arises when you take the lid off a can of adhesive or spread it on a surface. Even a small amount can make many people feel dizzy or sick. This is an indication of the strength of those fumes.

Anyone who finds themselves feeling really unwell after, say, laying floor tiles, has probably only themselves to blame. Had they bothered to read the manufacturer's instructions printed clearly on the side of the container they would have read explicit instructions to ensure maximum ventilation when working with the adhesives.

So that really is the starting point. Many people will read the instructions only after the adhesive has failed to stick properly. They then go over the instructions and notice the paragraph headed WARNING. This is the most vital part of the words on the container. Yet many people still do not read them. You may find a

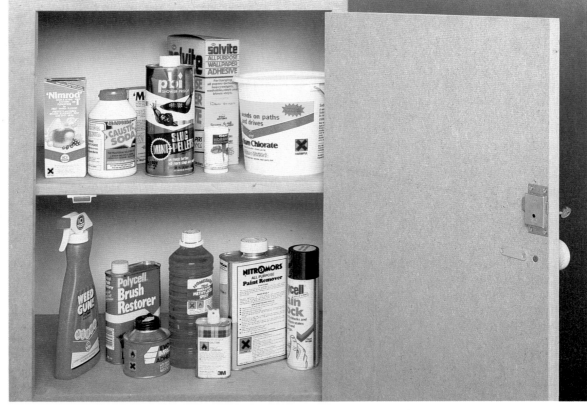

Keep garden and domestic chemicals locked away securely and keep the key in a safe place. Liquids should always be stored below solids so that if a bottle breaks the liquid cannot flow on to the packets of solids and damage them or, worse still, start a dangerous chemical reaction.

brief summary on the container with a leaflet giving full advice inside. Read this through completely – it takes only a few minutes and is time very well spent.

It is a good idea to tie the instructions to the container – especially if you live in a house where boxes are discarded quickly.

Everyone should make a point of reading the manufacturer's advice in its entirety before taking the lid off a product. You *must* know how to use the product correctly and safely. Never imagine that all adhesives are the same – they are not.

Ventilation

When ventilation is recommended, open wide as many windows as you can in the room. If possible open an outside door. It is probably best to close off doors leading to other parts of the house since fumes can carry into other rooms.

When the job is finished, replace the lid or cap and leave the windows or door open for a couple of hours to allow the fumes to dissipate.

Fumes can also be highly dangerous – they can be sufficiently volatile to ignite if they come into contact with a naked flame. So you may well find your instructions advising you to extinguish pilot lights from boilers, gas stoves, and so on that are in the vicinity. It will then also tell you not to smoke – a note pinned to the door will warn other smokers to keep away while you are working.

Fumes will also permeate clothes so, immediately you have finished, change into something clean and hang your working clothes out in the fresh air for a couple of hours before washing them. Do not wander into other rooms since you will be taking the fumes with you and, at the very least, you could inflict a feeling of nausea on others.

Cyanoacrylates – 'super-glues' to most people – must be treated with great respect. They are tremendously powerful and stick instantly. Since it is possible for a container to burst and squirt liquid into the face it is advisable to wear a mask and safety specs when using them.

On the side of the container will be first-aid advice to be followed in the event of an emergency. You must know what this is in advance. In a panic situation you do not want to try to find out what has to be done.

Obviously any chemical which is likely to be splashed around – such as wood-preservative or paint-stripper – can find its way onto parts of the skin. This can be extremely irritating or painful and will need to be washed off immediately. So the answer when brushing or spraying is to wear the correct safety gear – overalls, mask and safety spectacles.

If you do get splashed get to the nearest tap straight away and let plenty of running water flow onto your affected part. If irritation or pain continues later then you must seek medical help.

Poisoning is a high risk factor with liquids. This can cause severe sickness, permanent disablement or death. Store bottles and containers under lock and key and in cupboards not accessible to children.

Never mix household cleaners – a chemical reaction can cause poisonous fumes to be given off.

Store liquids in their original containers only. If a small quantity has to be transferred to a separate container for convenience while working, make sure it is clearly labelled and is not left unguarded at any time. After use, pour surplus liquid back into its original container, throw it away, or keep it stored in its new labelled container with the lid tightly fixed.

Glue guns

Finally, a word about glue guns. which are still fairly new to the d-i-y market. These are highly efficient but can be very dangerous. The idea is that glue sticks are melted by heat inside the gun and this, in liquid form, is then applied to the materials being stuck. Appearances can be very deceptive – it is hard for young children to appreciate how hot and sticky the molten glue can be – so keep them well away.

Hazard Symbols

Harmful substances are those which are dangerous to the skin. Irritants give off vapours or gases that are dangerous to inhale.

Harmful

Toxic covers solids, liquids or gases that are poisonous if swallowed or inhaled, even in tiny quantities (very toxic).

Toxic

Flammability increases with the ability of a flammable liquid to form a vapour. Lighter fuel and nail varnish remover are common examples.

Highly flammable

Explosives most likely to be encountered are fireworks. They must be stored in a dry cool place and, obviously, away from naked flames.

Explosive

Corrosives include acids (even weak ones such as vinegar) and alkalis such as washing soda. Never mix the two together.

Corrosive

Hydrogen peroxide and weedkiller (sodium chlorate) are common oxidisers which can release large quantities of oxygen to add 'fuel' to fires.

Oxidising

USING TOOLS

Buying the best tools you can afford and looking after them properly is excellent, traditional advice. There is no doubt that good tools, in the right hands, will produce top quality work. However, it matters little how much you pay for something if it is not right for you or if you fail to use it and look after it properly. You will not produce good work and, more important, you will also be putting yourself and those around you at risk. In other chapters you can find out how to keep tools sharp and the kind of protective safety clothes that are available. Here we are concerned with using tools correctly.

Power tools

There is no doubt that electric tools bring more power to your elbow – enabling anyone, weak or strong, to cut, shape or drill accurately and easily through the toughest materials – but they can be lethal. Each year many people receive serious cuts in their own home because they have not obeyed some simple rules, or have not been concentrating on what they are doing. It takes only a fraction of a second for an enjoyable job to become a disaster

Whenever you buy a power tool the first thing you should do when you unpack it is to study the manufacturer's instructions and get to know it. Get used to handling it, familiarize yourself with the instructions, understand the dangers associated with it. Then, and only then, you can fit a plug to the flex (again following the instruction label attached to it) and try it out.

There are some general rules which apply to each type of power tool, irrespective of whether it is a drill, saw or planer.

First of all, do keep children, animals and anyone else likely to interfere well away whenever a power tool is being used. If there are young children in the house, then always unplug a power tool if you have to leave a room. In many homes it is difficult to ensure that a toddler will stay out of a room and a power tool that is plugged in can be operated easily by inquisitive little hands.

Should you have to change a blade of a powersaw or the twist bit in a drill then switch off at the mains and unplug first. You might imagine that nothing could possibly happen to turn on the machine at the wrong moment, but a sudden distraction – a knock at the door, the sound of something or someone falling in another room – is all that it takes to momentarily divert your attention and you could inadvertently switch on while grasping a blade.

If you have to carry a tool around, do not carry it by the cable – it can easily cause a wiring problem.

If you have to use a power tool when you are off the ground make absolutely certain that your ladder, stepladder or trestle board is solidly positioned. If possible have a helper on the ground below to switch on the power only when you have reached your working position and are ready to begin. While you are working make sure no one is standing below in case the power tool should be accidently dropped. The other thing to remember is that the flex can

When using a circular saw, use a guide batten and keep both hands firmly in position.

Use a push-stick to feed the workpiece into the blade, and an offcut to hold it against the fence.

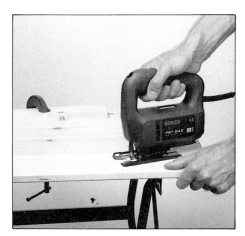

Always ensure that the workpiece is clamped firmly when working with power tools.

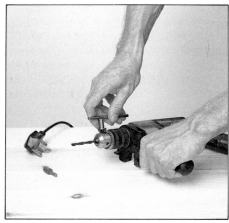

Whenever adjusting a power tool, switch off and unplug it from the socket. Ensure blades and bits are fitted securely.

easily get tangled up in your feet and cause a fall. There is a lot to think about when working high up with power equipment.

A power circuit breaker is essential when working with a lawnmower – that seems to be generally considered as the only use for this invaluable piece of equipment. Yet it can be just as much of a lifesaver with any piece of power equipment should the flex be cut. So get into the habit of plugging in to safety whenever you use a power tool.

Naturally it goes without saying (or does it?) that you should not use power equipment out of doors if it is raining.

In factories there are strict rules about what people are allowed to wear while operating machinery. They are sensible guidelines and it is important that the householder should think in the same terms at home. The golden rule is not to wear loose clothing or jewellery which could get caught in a moving part of a power tool. Long hair is equally dangerous so tie this back tightly.

You should always make sure that your workpiece is well anchored down – if it is able to move then you cannot be sure in which direction a power tool will suddenly go. So use workbench clamps or a vice to secure the workpiece. Similarly in other situations – when working on a door, for example, either close it or wedge it underneath to stop it moving.

A couple of points to note especially are that you should also engage a safety guard before operating a power saw and you must keep your hands and the flex behind the line of operation. Do not try to apply force to a power tool to make it work more quickly – apart from anything else you will damage it. If you are drilling or sawing through something then make sure there is nothing underneath which can be damaged or might damage the tool.

Hired tools

There is a vast array of weird and wonderful equipment which you can

A safety harness ensures that a power-tool flex does not risk being cut through.

obtain from hire shops. When you hire something you may be unfamiliar with how to use it properly. If this is the case then make sure that an assistant in the shop is able to tell you exactly how it works or is able to provide manufacturer's written instructions. If you have doubts about any particular point then make sure you have the information before leaving the shop. Get a telephone number and if necessary, telephone for information if a problem arises at home.

A lot of powerful hired equipment must be used in conjunction with protective clothing. Ask about this at the same time that you hire it.

Although 'professional' equipment brings a greater scope of jobs within your reach it does not follow that you have the necessary knowledge to handle the job safely.

A chimney scaffold, for example, makes working on the stack very safe but you still have to know how to carry the pieces properly in order to get them up to the roof and erected safely. Then, although you may be well capable of repointing the brickwork or even resetting new pots in cement flaunching, you may not be equipped to dismantle an old

and heavy stack.

The chainsaw, being so efficient, has become an extremely popular item but you have to remember just how dangerous it can be. The blade can cause extensive injury should it kick-back in use or should the log being sawn suddenly give way allowing the saw blade to travel on towards your leg.

Just because you have a chainsaw, it does not mean you can cut down a tree or even lop off a few branches. Felling a tree means being off the ground which is not the place for an amateur to be with a chainsaw. You are better off with an alternative such as a pruning saw or a logsaw. Confine your chainsaw use to cutting up logs on the ground. Do use wedges to stop the log rolling around and also be prepared to drive wedges into the saw cut so that it doesn't close on the saw blade causing it to jam. Only cut downwards, using the flat part of the chain – never the end of the chain.

Going back to tree felling for a moment, whatever you use, felling a large tree is not work for an amateur. A single tree branch, once cut through, can cause havoc if it does not fall correctly. Even a fairly thin-

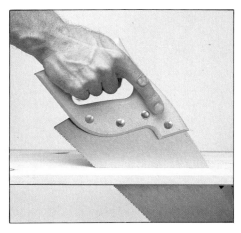

Hold a saw firmly with the index finger pointing in the direction of the cut along the handle.

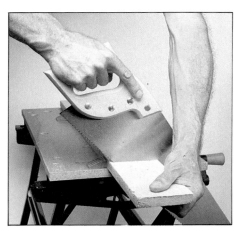

Always support the offcut towards the end of the cut to prevent the saw from suddenly breaking clear.

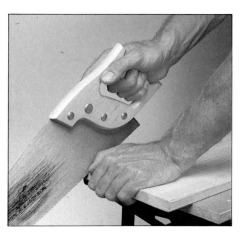

Keep a firm grip on the workpiece when starting the cut and saw gently to prevent the blade from jumping.

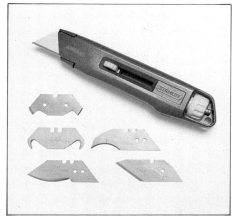

A trimming knife with a rectractable blade is the safest. Always use the correct blade for the material being cut.

Use a wedge to prevent the cut closing and jamming the saw abruptly, which can cause the blade to kink or twist.

If a screwdriver blade is too narrow, it can be forced clear of the slot suddenly when under pressure.

looking branch can be impossibly heavy – especially when falling. The skill of tree felling is in knowing exactly how and where to make cuts, and how to secure branches with ropes before sawing through them. In short, for all but the simplest jobs, call in the experts.

Hand tools

Whereas there is more reason to think automatically in terms of safety when reaching for a power tool, it is easy to become complacent when working with the more familiar hammer or panel saw. Yet in their own way, hand tools can be equally dangerous.

First, you must always take the trouble to look after hand tools – do not discard a tool you have finished using by throwing it carelessly into the toolbag – treat it as a carpenter would treat his treasured tools. Then correct and safe use of them will become second nature.

In general, always keep tools sharp and clean and store them in dry conditions so that they will not rust. Saws and knives are usually supplied with a blade cover. Look after this and keep it on the saw teeth or edge of the blade always – whether the tool is kept hanging up in the garage or with everything else in the tool bag.

Whenever you are going to use a saw, the first thing to do is to secure the workpiece, however large or small. Position it so that the cut line just overhangs the edge of the bench, to ensure maximum support and prevent whip.

Get your feet into a comfortable, firm stance and position yourself so that the saw becomes an extension of your arm with your index finger pointing in the direction of the cut. Do not saw in a jerky movement: draw the saw cleanly back and forth through the cut remembering that you cut on the forward stroke only.

When you get near the end of the cut, make sure that the workpiece is supported on both sides of the cut line and make the final cuts slowly, short in length and gently. If you

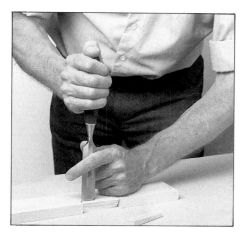

When chopping with a chisel, guide it between thumb and finger.

When using a chisel, keep your guiding hand behind the leading edge.

A screwdriver is a harmless object but it can still be misused. The blade tip of a standard screwdriver should be clean and square so that it engages the screw slot perfectly. The first thing to do is to select the correct width blade for the screw slot being turned. The screw slot itself should be clean as well – showing no build up of paint or dirt. If you have the wrong size screwdriver then it can slip out of the slot, especially on a tight turn, causing a cut on your other hand – and damaging the work surface to add insult to injury!

Chisels are extremely dangerous if blunt or misused. It is essential that the workpiece should be well secured before starting. You can use

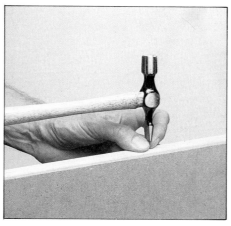

Small pins can be driven safely with the peen of a pin-hammer.

If you do not have the proper hammer use a piece of card to support the pin initially.

A cable and pipe detector will ensure that you do not have any nasty surprises when drilling into a wall.

a mallet or hammer (with a plastic-handled chisel) to take away the bulk of the wood, but final paring is always done under hand pressure only. Use the fingers of your spare hand to steady and guide the blade.

Everyone knows that a hammer can cause a bruised thumb – it is something of a music-hall joke, but only when it happens to others. When you buy a hammer, get one that you can use comfortably. A heavy hammer is better only if you can strike a nail cleanly with it.

When you bang in a nail, always be well positioned and standing firmly. Start off with gentle blows, gradually increasing the strength until you are working with a positive, flowing movement.

Do not take your eye off the nail from start to finish. If a nail is difficult to grasp at first, push it through a piece of card about 75mm (3in) long and use this to hold it in place initially. Pull away the card just before delivering the final blows.

Bruised thumbs are mostly caused by the hammer slipping off the nail as it is struck. One reason is that the face of the hammer is dirty or greasy. Keep a scrap piece of coarse abrasive paper in your tool kit and remember to rub over the face occasionally to keep it clean and slightly rough so that it will have some degree of grip.

continue to saw at a rapid rate you risk having no control over the direction of the saw as it bursts through the material.

A sharp knife is an essential part of a tool kit for a number of jobs involving a lot of materials. Make sure that the blade is kept sharp and that you use the correct blade for the material being cut, whether it is paper, floor tiles or carpet. Remember to keep your fingers out of the line of the cut and do not exert too much pressure or the blade may slip sideways.

The safest type of knife is one with a retractable blade. A small button on the body of the knife slides back to pull the blade inside so that it is safely stored until needed again.

SHARPENING TOOLS

If you ask which is the more dangerous, a blunt chisel or a sharp one, many people will opt for the sharp one. In fact it is the blunt one that is more likely to slip away from the workpiece and cut the user – and a 'blunt' chisel can cause a severe injury. A good DIYer keeps cutting tools as sharp as a razor. It takes less energy to sharpen your tools than it does to work with blunt ones – just try cutting along a plank with a blunt saw. You cannot make a clean, accurate cut with a blunt saw; and it is almost impossible to get a tenon to fit snugly inside a mortise if you are using a chisel with a dull edge.

There is a variety of ingenious gadgets readily available for accurate honing of chisels, spoke-shaves and plane blades. Electric-powered grindstones enable you to use both hands to do the job and they spin with almost no vibration, so accurate results can be achieved without fuss; drill bit sharpeners can save you money in the long run and oilstones are vital to every toolkit.

Oilstones

There are many natural and man-made stones with different grit sizes and densities for sharpening tools such as chisels and planes.

Coarse stones are used to regrind old or damaged tools, the medium grits are for sharpening and the high-density natural stones with the finer grit sizes are for the final honing. For the average do-it-yourselfer a combination stone is the best bet: these usually have a medium face on one side and a fine face on the other. Coarse stones are required only when the blade of a tool is badly chipped or worn and large amounts of steel have to be removed before the final sharpening and honing.

When the surface of an oilstone becomes clogged with dirt and oil, wash it vigorously with a scrubbing brush and paraffin; when it becomes hollowed, sprinkle some carborundum powder on a sheet of glass and rub the surface of the stone over it until it is ground flat. Keep the oilstone in a box (make your own if it is not supplied) and put a few drops of light lubricating oil on it every time before use. Use the entire surface to avoid uneven wear.

Slipstones

Like oilstones, slipstones are for putting the final razor-sharp edge on cutting tools but they are specially shaped to fit irregular cutting edges on tools such as gouges and the V-shaped chisels used by woodcarvers. The most common slipstones are rectangular, triangular and circular.

Honing guides

Look at the blade of a chisel or plane and you will see that two angles form the cutting edge; the long, ground face slopes back at 25 degrees but the tip is honed to 30 degrees. It takes a lot of practice to do a good job of this so a honing guide is invaluable since it takes the guesswork out of the process, ensuring perfect results. It can be used for firmer and bevel edge chisels and plane blades, from 2mm ($\frac{1}{16}$in) to 65mm ($2\frac{5}{8}$in) wide.

It is very simple to use: the amount the blade being sharpened projects from the honing guide determines the angle and these projections are embossed on the side of the tool so the operating instructions cannot be lost. Once you have bought one you will wonder how you ever managed without it.

If you happen to chip the cutting edge of a chisel against a piece of metal, for example a nail or screw, then it will have to be reground against a grinding wheel. Hold the edge against the tool rest and move it back and forwards against the cutting wheel until the chip is removed and the edge is clean. Do not

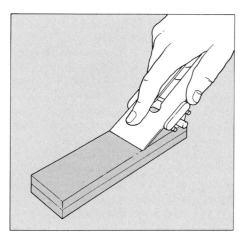

A honing guide, used on an oilstone, ensures carefully sharpened angles on chisels and planes.

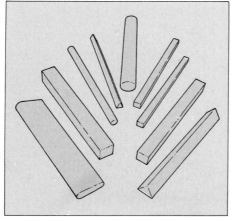

Slipstones sharpen smaller tools and shaped tools which cannot be sharpened to an oilstone.

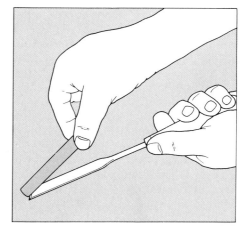

Choose a slipstone that fits the inside curve of a gouge and remove any burr on a flat stone.

lean heavily on the chisel. Keep it cool by dipping it in water.

Saw tooth setter

After a lot of use, even the best quality saws become blunt and the tooth set worn; this causes the saw to wander from the cutting line and jam in the cut. But taking your saw to the 'saw doctor' will take the edge off your bank balance; a saw set and saw sharpener (always used together) enable you to avoid the doctor's bills and do the job yourself.

The saw set can be used to reset the teeth of most wood saws (with the exception of hardpoint saws); the amount of set is adjustable and the tool is straightforward to use.

Saws have certain number of teeth to the inch – the greater number, the finer the cut. (If you do not know the numbers, just count them.) Adjust the saw set to this number and position it over the first tooth pointing away from the set. Then squeeze the handles of the set together and that tooth will be accurately aligned. Work along the full length of the saw setting each tooth pointing away from you – that is, every other tooth. When you get to the end, turn the saw around and work backwards on the other teeth until they have all been bent to the correct angle.

Saw sharpener

The sharpener can be used on almost all wood saws (except hardpoint saws) and is designed in such a way that you really cannot go wrong; you select the amount of metal to be removed, and a triangular file rolls on two guide bars ensuring uniformity of tooth shape and sharpness.

Drill sharpeners

The hand-operated drill sharpener is a great device for the average do-it-yourselfer – it is economical and it puts an edge on twist drills which are expensive to renew.

It is simple to use and takes carbon or high-speed drills from 3mm (⅛in) to 13mm (½in). To restore a sharp edge quickly, position the drill bit securely in the shaft of the tool then roll the sharpener over abrasive paper (provided).

You can also get drill bit sharpening attachments for power drills. They are suitable for most types of power drill (but you should check) and it is recommended that a drill stand should also be used. They are very quick and easy to use: it is just a matter of inserting the drill bit into the corresponding diameter hole in the top of the attachment.

Grinding wheels

They come in a wide variety of sizes and in many different grades of grit, from coarse to smooth; coarse grits for regrinding damaged blades, medium and fine grits for sharpening. They can be used in power drill attachments, in bench grinders (single or double) or hand grinders (inconvenient to use with one hand only). They are invaluable for grinding centre punches, scissors, and cold chisels, for repairing screwdriver tips, for regrinding and sharpening drill bits, chisels and plane blades and for putting a keen edge back on dull garden tools. You can get green grits which will put a keen edge on tungsten carbide tipped tools.

Always wear goggles to protect your eyes and follow the manufacturer's instructions carefully when using power devices.

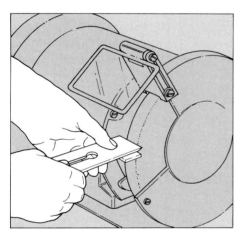

If a chisel or plane blade gets chipped, it must be reground using a grinding wheel.

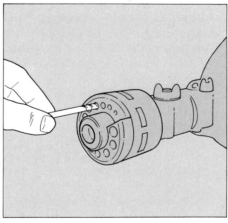

An electric drill sharpener will put a new cutting edge on a wide range of drill bit sizes.

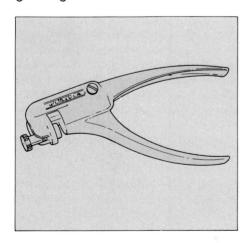

A saw tooth setter bends back the teeth to the correct angle, so preventing the the blade from binding.

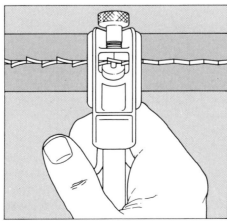

Position the set over alternative teeth and squeeze the handles firmly together.

GLASS

Glass is everywhere around us in our homes: windows, shelves, mirrors, table tops, display cabinets, pictures and so on. Nowadays it comes in many different forms and patterns which can offer extra benefits and, more important, extra safety. To take advantage of this you need to know the right type of glass to use in any particular situation.

Ordinary glass, used correctly, is perfectly safe. It is only when it is broken that danger arises. So find out here what type you should be using — and where. If you discover a danger spot in your home, fit the right glass — right now.

Glass used to be supplied by weight – i.e., 24oz or 32oz. This has now been replaced by metric thicknesses ranging from 3mm to 10mm according to use.

Glass types

Sheet glass A cheap glass with imperfections. Often referred to as horticultural glass, it is used for glazing greenhouses and frames. Sheet thickness is 3mm (⅛in) which is the equivalent of the old 24oz glass. Never use it for domestic glazing – or for double glazing.

Float glass This is flat and free from imperfections, so it is the material used for domestic glazing. It is available in thicknesses from 3mm to 10mm, the 4mm thickness being equivalent to the old 32oz glass.

Thickness must be related to the size of window. For example:

Window size	Glass
up to 6sq.ft	3mm
up to 12sq.ft	4mm
up to 16sq.ft	5mm
up to 25sq.ft	6mm
up to 50sq.ft	10mm

These thicknesses are only a guide. For unusual conditions, such as high wind pressures, allowances must be made. Also, certain areas at risk need safety glass (see toughened and laminated glass).

When buying glass for shelves, ask your supplier to smooth the edges for you.

Patterned glass A smooth glass with a pattern rolled on to one side. When used for glazing exterior windows and doors, the smooth side always goes outside so that the putty has a flat surface to bond to, to keep the weather out. It varies in thickness from 3mm to 5mm and it admits about 75 per cent of the light transmitted through a clear sheet.

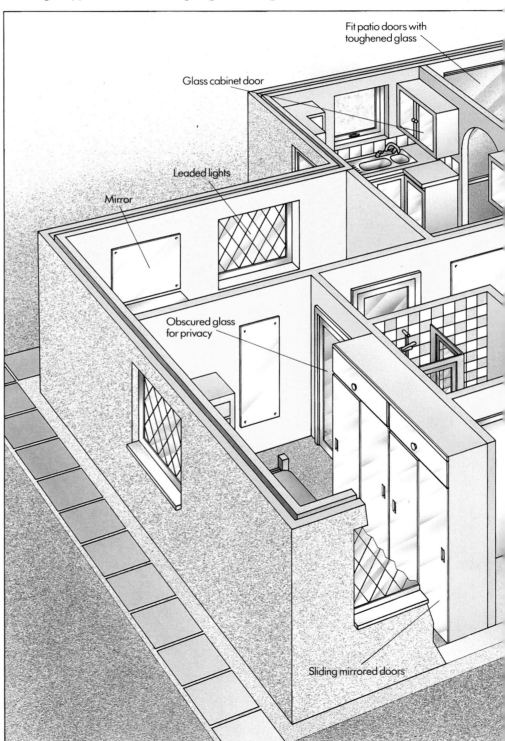

Fit patio doors with toughened glass

Glass cabinet door

Leaded lights

Mirror

Obscured glass for privacy

Sliding mirrored doors

Solar control glass Now popular in double-glazing, it is a float glass which has a fine mirror coating applied which reflects the sun's rays while not affecting visibility through the glass. It may be clear or slightly tinted. During winter it will help keep warmth in a room, increasing the effect of double glazing by about 20 per cent.

Wired glass A rolled glass which has a wire mesh embedded in it during manufacture. It is 6mm thick, with a choice of square or diamond-pattern mesh. Under impact, the wire holds the glass together. It is often used where fire-resistance is important and on glazed roofs where ice or snow is likely to drop on it. Despite its strength, it is not recommended for security glazing as the mesh can be broken through once the glass has been smashed. Be sure to order the correct size when using it for glazing as it is difficult to trim or cut.

Laminated glass This is formed by two sheets of float glass with a thin sheet of crystal-clear plastic sandwiched between. It is very strong. Under heavy impact the glass will crack but the plastic holds it very firmly together. This glass is specified for areas of high risk and for security glazing.

Laminated glass is now available through local glaziers and it can be cut to size (unlike toughened glass).

Toughened glass Sometimes referred to as armour-plate glass, this glass has both impact and fire-resistance. This means that once it has been toughened it cannot be cut to size, so it must be ordered to exact measurements. When it does break it shatters into hundreds of small but harmless pieces. It is used in areas of risk, such as for balcony glazing, and is also supplied as complete glazed doors.

Mirrored glass This type is available in a number of thicknesses, both in sheet and tile form. Where damp is likely to be encountered – such as in the bathroom – special damp-resisting backings are available. It is possible to cut mirror glass, but it is not easy to get a smooth edge to the mirror finish on the back. It is sometimes possible to hide the edge by framing.

Plate glass This is very expensive now, so is little used domestically. Float glass has taken its place, using the 5mm to 10mm thicknesses.

Picture frame glass Usually 2mm or 3mm thick, glass is available with diffuse reflection, making it ideal for pictures which are illuminated or which are likely to pick up reflections from a nearby window.

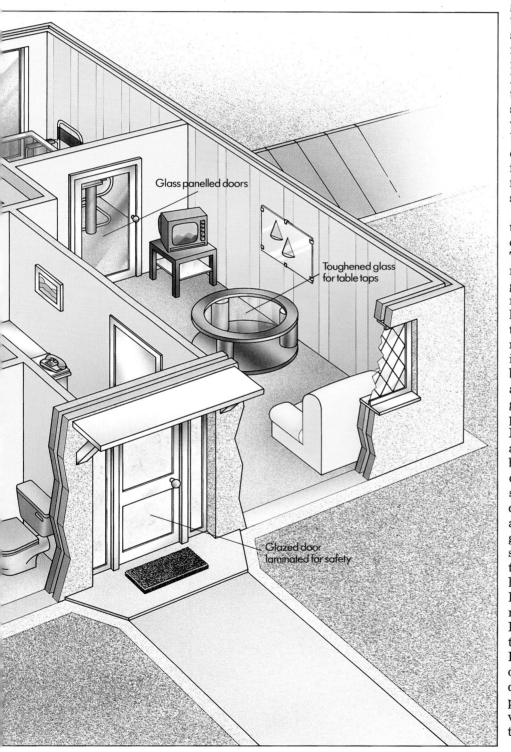

Glass panelled doors

Toughened glass for table tops

Glazed door laminated for safety

Replacing a pane of glass

When a window breaks the immediate priority is to remove every fragment. Keep children and pets well away until every piece has been swept up and deposited in the dustbin in a protective covering, if necessary in a separate container and labelled. Wear a pair of old leather gloves whenever handling broken glass.

Start taking out pieces from along the top of the frame, then work down the sides, finishing along the bottom. Then deal with stubborn pieces. Run a glass cutter around the perimeter of the glass, close to the rebates. Then tap out the pieces with a light hammer handle, holding each piece until it is free.

Any putty can be chopped away using a hacking knife or chisel, and final fragments removed.

Having removed the putty you will see a series of small nails, called sprigs, which do the real job of retaining the glass. Remove these with pincers. If they are removed carefully and are straight they can be reused. If not, buy some new ones.

With metal frames there will be special clips rather than sprigs. These can usually be removed carefully for reuse. Mark their positions around the rebate. One arm slots into a hole in the rebate, the other clamps on the face of the glass.

The glass may have been secured by wood beading fixed with panel pins. Usually these cannot be seen.

Prise the beading away carefully and remove the pins. Take care not to damage the beading.

Brush away all dust from the rebates then apply a coat of suitable primer. Now you can measure up and order the new glass, putty and, if necessary, sprigs or clips.

Measuring up

Accurate measuring for the new sheet of glass is vital. Measure the full width of the opening between the rebates at the top, centre and bottom. If there is a difference note down the *smallest* of the measurements. Next, measure from top to bottom between the rebates following the same procedure. Finally, deduct 3mm (⅛in) from the smallest

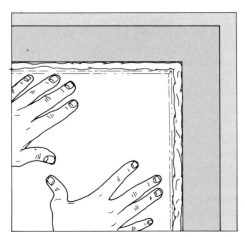

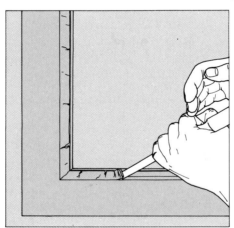

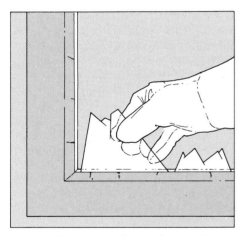

1 Wiggle out broken glass; gloves must be worn.

2 Remove hard putty with an old chisel.

3 Brush all dust from rebates to ensure good adhesion.

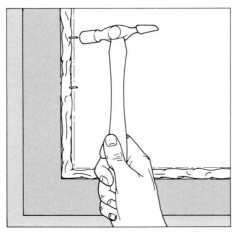

6 Press the new pane into place — around the edges only.

7 Use a small hammer or square-edge chisel to tap in sprigs.

8 Angle putty neatly with wet putty knife. Paint after at least a week.

height and width measurements (the ones you have noted). These are the dimensions to hand to your supplier. The reason for deducting 3mm is that glass tends to expand and contract in the frame.

If a frame is badly out of square or an awkward shape the safest thing to do is to make a cardboard pattern and hand this to your supplier.

Take some old newspapers with you, or your gloves, to protect your hands from the edge of the glass when you are carrying it.

Buy the correct putty – linseed-oil putty for timber frames; metal-casement putty for metal frames. If new sprigs are needed buy 15mm (⅝in) long types.

The putty must be soft and pli-able. If it is hard, then it can be made workable by rolling it in small pieces in your hands. You can add a little linseed oil to standard putty to make it more pliable. Wetting your hands in water before handling putty will prevent it from sticking to your fingers.

Fitting the glass

Around the rebate run a continuous layer of soft putty about 3mm (⅛in) thick. Press it well into place with your thumb.

Carefully raise the glass into position, allowing for the 3mm expansion gap all round. Press the glass firmly into the bed of putty, applying pressure only on the edges of the glass – never in the middle.

Now refit the sprigs or clips. Sprigs are placed at intervals of about 15cm (6in) around the glass. They must lie flush with the glass to retain it securely, so tap them in carefully using the side of a chisel as a hammer. Refit clips in their original positions.

Run a final layer of putty around the outside of the glass, pressing it in with the thumb. Smooth out the layer with a putty knife and form neat mitres at the corners. Smooth and angle the putty to match that on surrounding windows. Keep the putty knife wet with water and the putty will not cling to it.

Use the edge of the knife to trim off surplus putty from both sides of the glass. Finally, run over the putty with a paintbrush dipped in water. This will make sure it adheres well to the glass making a tight seal to prevent rainwater penetration.

Paint over the putty after a week to fourteen days.

Emergency repair

If you break a window during an evening or weekend when you cannot get new glass, you may have to make a temporary repair, especially if the window is vulnerable to intruders or bad weather.

Use a sheet of polythene, which will keep out the elements but still allow light through, and fix it to the inside of the window. During warm weather it will probably be sufficient to stretch the polythene tightly over the opening and to secure it with adhesive tape.

In the winter a more substantial fixing for the polythene will be needed. First, using drawing pins, secure the top of the polythene to the window frame. Then nail a timber batten along the top to hold it tight. Use a batten to secure both sides and another to finish along the bottom edge. Stretch the polythene as you work to smooth out wrinkles caused by uneven tension.

Polythene has no security value so, if the window offers easy access to the house, nail a sheet of hardboard or plywood instead.

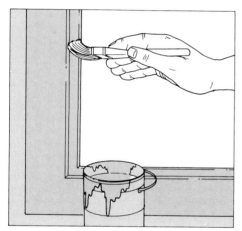

4 Check frame for square and apply suitable primer.

5 Run a layer of putty around the frame rebate.

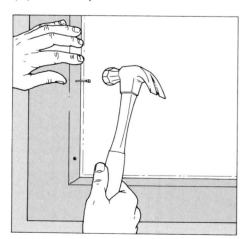

9 When using beading, mitre the corners and pin in place.

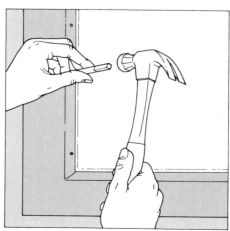

10 Drive pin heads below surface with a nail punch and hammer.

ELECTRICITY

Numerous fatalities occur each year due to electrocutions caused by faulty wiring or by misuse of appliances, in many cases leading to house fires.

When you move into a 'new' home your surveyor's report should give a complete assessment of the state of the electrical system. It is then up to you to act immediately to correct any faults highlighed, which might entail complete rewiring.

If you do jobs yourself, ensure that you know precisely what is involved before you start and observe the rules and safety precautions. If you have the slightest doubt, call in the professionals.

Of all the parts in a house it is the electrical system that presents the average householder with the biggest problem in terms of understanding how it works. However, a basic knowledge of the electrical installation will enable you to assess whether rewiring is required, and it will enable you to carry out basic maintenance and improvements. Remember: ALWAYS TURN OFF THE MAIN SWITCH BEFORE INSPECTING OR WORKING ON ANY ELECTRICAL CIRCUIT.

A quick inspection will give you a pretty good idea of the condition of your house electrical system.

A modern installation will have 13 amp (square pin) socket outlets, whereas the old-fashioned sockets had two or three round pins.

This in itself is not a foolproof test; the modern sockets could have been connected up to old wiring. Broken socket covers and other damage will be obvious. Examine closely for any scorching around socket pin holes which show that the plug has overheated at some time.

You can get 13 amp sockets with or without switches. Switched types are better because they have an on/off control switch which means that the power to the socket can be switched off before plugging in, or unplugging, an appliance. The basic type has a red cap on the switch which becomes visible when the switch is on.

Socket outlets should be fixed 450mm (18in) above floor level. This prevents the flex being bent, and

possibly damaged which could happen when connecting a plug to a socket fixed to a skirting board.

You are not allowed to have a socket outlet in the bathroom. This is because of the obvious risk of electrocution from portable heating appliances and the lethal combination of water and electricity.

Perfect-looking sockets, light switches and ceiling roses can be covering a dangerous situation. Unscrew the cover and pull it forward to inspect the wiring. The wires should be plastic covered and flex easily without breaking. If they are brittle and crack easily then heat inside the socket may have caused them to perish. Again, not foolproof, but a good indication for the need to but indication of the need to rewire.

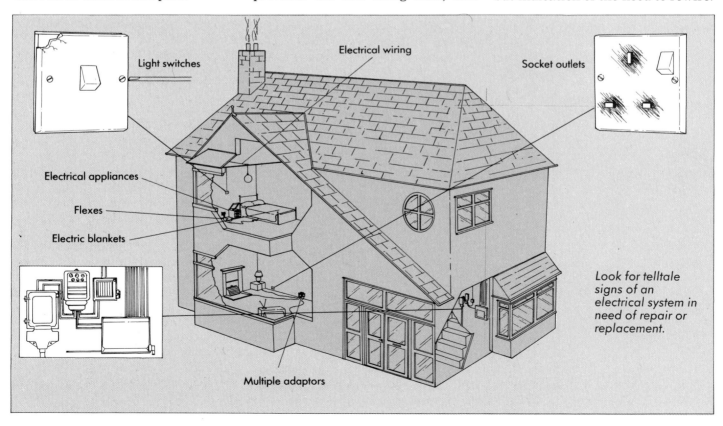

Light switches

Electrical wiring

Socket outlets

Electrical appliances

Flexes

Electric blankets

Multiple adaptors

Look for telltale signs of an electrical system in need of repair or replacement.

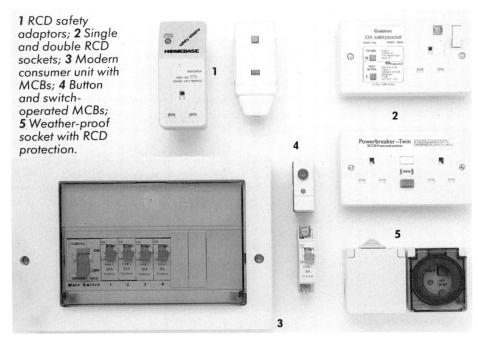

1 RCD safety adaptors; 2 Single and double RCD sockets; 3 Modern consumer unit with MCBs; 4 Button and switch-operated MCBs; 5 Weather-proof socket with RCD protection.

Take up a floorboard below a socket outlet and have a look at the condition of the cable down below. If it is flat, pvc and grey or white, it is modern and should be in good condition. Lead-covered cable or plain black or white rubber is obsolete.

What is the main control of your electrical system like? (This is usually found in an understairs or hall cupboard.) A modern consumer unit indicates reasonably new wiring. A collection of separate boxes with switches, or an old-style fuse-box with a switch, together with a jumble of wires, shows an old-style system in need of modernisation.

The electricity supply cable from outside runs into the consumer unit bringing power to the house. From there it is distributed around the house through wiring circuits. Each wiring circuit has its own fuse in the consumer unit.

Circuit fuses

There are two types of circuit fuses fitted into consumer units: the rewirable or semi-enclosed type and the cartridge type. They are made in five current ratings and are colour coded: 5 amp (white); 15 amp (blue); 20 amp (yellow); 30 amp (red); 45 amp (green).

Both types are fitted into fuse carriers which plug into the fuse-ways of the consumer unit. The fuse wire is the fuse element of the rewirable type. A cartridge fuse has a silver fuse element enclosed in a ceramic cartridge filled with quartz (sand) and has a metal cap at each end which makes contact with the fuse-way contacts. The cartridges are different sizes according to the rating, except the 15 and 20 amp ratings which are the same.

Mending a rewirable fuse

Turn off the main switch and pull out the relevant carrier having first checked the circuit list on the cover of the consumer unit. If there is no list it is necessary to check each fuse of the current rating relevant to the faulty circuit. Select the correct fuse wire from the card and cut off sufficient length. Next, remove any bits of old fuse wire and any blobs of copper from the carrier.

Insert the end of the fuse wire in the ceramic or asbestos tube and connect it to the carrier terminal. Connect the other end of the fuse wire to the other terminal taking care not to strain the wire placed clockwise under the washer of a clamp-type screw. Trim off any sur-

plus wire and insert the carrier into the consumer unit. Replace the consumer unit cover and switch on.

If the fuse blows immediately, the fault has not cleared, which indicates the problem is serious and requires professional attention.

Replacing cartridge fuses

A cartridge fuse cannot be rewired and no attempt must be made to do so. Nor must a substitute be fitted where no replacement is available. Having attempted to locate the fault, remove the carrier from the consumer unit and take out the fuse. Fit a new fuse of the same colour and current rating.

Replace the carrier in the consumer unit. Put back the cover and turn on the main switch.

If the new cartridge does not blow immediately the fault was a transient one, such as the surge of current upon the failure of a light bulb.

The alternative to fuses in the consumer unit is miniature circuit breakers (MCBs). These automatically switch off when there is a fault or overload on the circuit. If you switch them back on, full power will be restored provided that the fault has been remedied on the circuit.

Some consumer units have a residual current device (RCD) (described below in more detail) instead of a main switch, for extra protection of the user.

Safety cut-out

When using electrical equipment you can guard against electrocution by plugging the appliance into an RCD socket or adaptor.

RCDs work by monitoring the current flowing to the appliance. Normally the current flowing in the live and neutral wires is equal, but the instant there is an imbalance such as when there is an earth leakage due to a fault or accident, this is instantly detected by the RCD, which automatically cuts off the power in a split second, before a tragedy can occur.

FIRE

It is terrifying to think of your house catching fire. The first smell of acrid, black smoke in the middle of the night, the panic, screams, flames, scrambling downstairs or getting to windows, fire engines, ambulances, police. Anyone who has personally experienced a serious fire in their own home will be able to tell you what a frightening ordeal it is.

At best you will have seen part of your home, together with treasured possessions, ruined. At worst you can lose loved ones. All fires starting inside a house are avoidable — they are caused through carelessness.

To prevent a fire it is vital to know how they are most likely to be caused. You should also know the kind of equipment to have in order to deal with one and what immediate action to take.

One thing should be understood about deaths caused by house fires — most victims are not burnt to death, they die from being overcome by smoke and fumes. They are then not in a position to get out of the building or to get to a window from where they can be rescued.

Let us look at the major causes of fires and see what can be done to eliminate them, starting with the simplest — smoking. The classic example is the overloaded ashtray, left smouldering as the last cigarette of the day is 'stubbed out'. Falling asleep while smoking either in a

Danger points:
A Flames up chip pan, projecting handle; B Towels drying; C Open window/curtains near cooker; D Flex over worktop edge; E Socket overload; F Frayed flex across floor; G Heater by chair; H, J Unguarded fire and clothes drying in front; K Smouldering cigarette. L TV left plugged in;

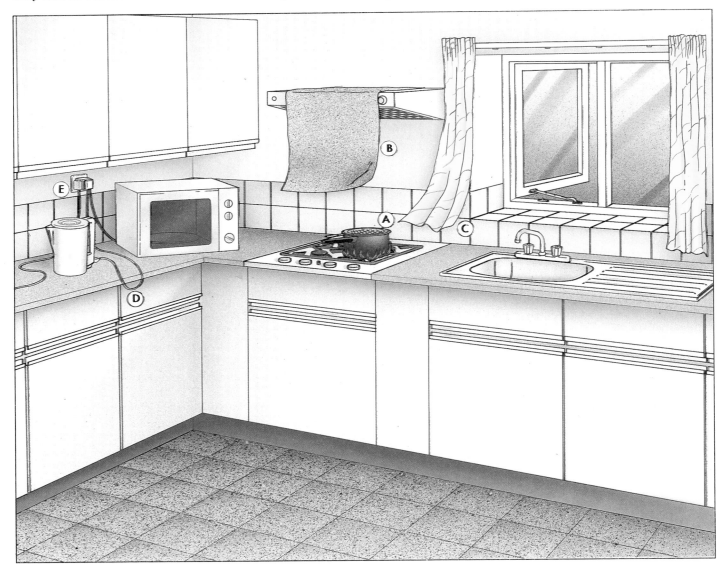

chair or in bed can have devastating consequences too. Or there may even be the carelessly discarded matchstick, still alight, thrown into a wastepaper basket.

Open fires and certain types of room heaters are obvious causes. Coals or logs can fall onto a carpet long after the family have gone to bed – which is why it is important to 'settle down' an open fire long before bedtime and make sure there is a hearth and fireguard. The latter will take care of any burning debris should any fall out during the course of the evening.

Other heaters, such as oil and paraffin stoves, are perfectly safe provided that they are maintained and handled correctly. They should never be moved around when alight and should be filled and lit in precise accordance with manufacturer's instructions. You should never leave children alone in a room with room heaters or open fires.

Perhaps it is the kitchen where most of us think that a fire will start. It is the burning chip pan which is the first obvious cause, though curtains billowing over the flames of a hob, or a tea towel carelessly placed on an electric ring can also be major reasons.

Probably the least thought-about cause of house fires is electric wiring. We are all aware (or should be!) of the dangers of electric blankets and of not unplugging television sets overnight and so on, but wiring is often overlooked. In the chapter on electricity you will find a useful guide to inspecting your electricity system to see if it is a risky proposition. Here it is worth stressing that sockets should never be overloaded – a temptation when adaptors are used.

Another bad practice which is very common is running flexes under carpets to prevent them trailing across the floor. This can cause them to heat up and ignite the carpet; it can smoulder for hours and only become a serious problem long after bedtime.

Do make it a habit always to re-

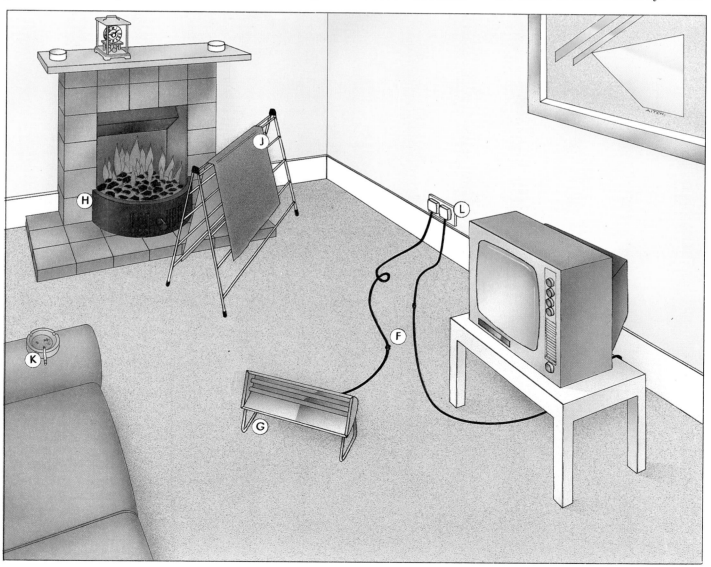

FITTING A SMOKE DETECTOR

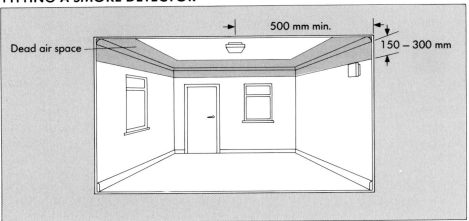

500 mm min.

Dead air space

150 – 300 mm

Correct positions for a smoke detector to avoid dead air space.

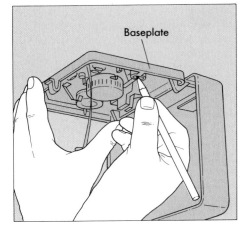

Baseplate

Fitting a smoke detector.

place a fuse with one of the correct rating should it blow.

Another sensible precaution is to make sure that all flammable liquids are stored safely. Never bring petrol into the house. It is vital never to smoke when using chemicals or adhesives since the vapours they give off can cause a fire.

Of course you can also inadvertently start a fire when doing DIY work. Using a blowtorch to burn off paint has been the cause of many a blaze. The typical situations are curtains getting caught alight inside an open window, or a bird's nest in the eaves starting to burn.

If you are soldering a joint in plumbing work then make sure you put a heat-resistant mat behind the joint – this will ensure that heat from the blowtorch does not ignite a skirting board or anything flammable in the vicinity.

Prevention products

One death in five in the home is attributed to upholstery fires, and the main culprit is the polyurethane foam filling which has been used in furniture manufacture since 1950. Recently there have been new regulations introduced concerning foam-filled furniture – under these new rules the use of untreated foam filling in the manufacture of furniture is prohibited. Householders who already own this type of furni-

ture and cannot afford to replace it can treat it with fire-retardant which can be sprayed on to furniture, fabrics, drapes, carpets, fabric roller blinds, rugs, mattresses etc., and offers immediate protection. It prevents fires by carbonizing at the heat source; this makes a thermal barrier which prevents heat penetration and ignition.

Smoke detectors

Once a fire breaks out in the home, findings show that 80 per cent of domestic fires burn for more than five minutes before they are discovered. Smoke detectors can provide extra minutes to escape safely.

They come in two forms: ionisation detectors, which are the most popular, and photoelectric units. The first type has a chamber enclosing two electrodes; when smoke particles enter the chamber, the current flow is reduced and the alarm is activated. These devices are particularly sensitive to fast-flaming fires. Photoelectric devices contain a light beam and a photoelectric cell; when the beam encounters smoke, the alarm is triggered. This type of alarm reacts very quickly to deep-smouldering fires of the kind experienced with furniture blazes.

There is a third category, which includes devices combining both photoelectric and ionisation techniques. Although more expensive,

they combine the best of both worlds and are a good investment.

Install alarms in rooms where an outbreak of fire is most likely, with the exception of bathrooms and kitchens where steam, or smoke from cooking, may trigger them.

A single alarm may be sufficient for a small house or bungalow but if your house has several levels it is sensible to place a detector on the ceiling of each landing. Make sure that the unit you choose conforms to BS 5446, Part 1. Some detectors have a number of extras, such as an escape light (invaluable if the electrics have been damaged), a low-battery indicator, and a test button to check that the alarm is working properly.

Fire extinguishers

When you buy an extinguisher make sure that every member of the family knows how to operate it. An emergency is no time to start reading the instructions on the side of the container. Domestic units can be effective against small fires, but they should be serviced at least once a year to guarantee reliable performance.

There are five types available:
Water extinguishers are suitable for fires which engulf paper or wood, but they should not be used on electrical appliances or on burning oil.
Foam extinguishers may be a better choice for most households – they

DEALING WITH A CHIP PAN FIRE

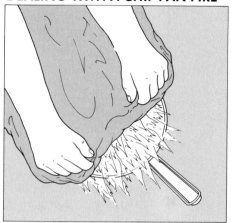

Correct use of a fire blanket.

can be used on flammable liquids, such as chip-pan fires. However, they are not suitable for use on live electrical appliances.

Vapourising liquid extinguishers (bfc or halon) score highly on most points. They can be used on all types of domestic fire and are clean to operate. On the minus side, they can adversely affect the user if operated in a confined space, so it is advisable to leave the scene once the product has been used.

Carbon dioxide extinguishers can

be used on both burning liquids and electrical appliances. Again, try to avoid using them in confined spaces as they can affect the operator.

Multi-purpose powder units are safe to use on most fires but they can be messy and difficult to clean up after. The product does not cool fires very successfully, and blazes can re-ignite.

Fire blankets

Blankets are ideal for smothering chip-pan fires, and for preventing further harm if clothing catches fire.

They are constructed of heavy, non-flammable materials which have good insulation properties, i.e. they will protect your hands from burns if held from above.

Keep your blanket within easy reach in case of an emergency – most come in a holder which can be mounted on the wall. The blanket is generally freed by two pull-cords and is ready for immediate use.

Emergency procedure

How you react when you are first aware of a fire is crucial. Much depends on the situation. If the fire is small, in a waste paper basket or a chip pan for instance, you may be

able to deal with it quickly. An extinguisher will take care of the wastepaper basket situations, and a fire blanket will put out the chip pan fire – but do turn off the heat and leave the pan where it is with the blanket over it for half-an-hour afterwards to give it time to cool down. Do not try and carry a blazing chip pan to safety. If the fire is too big to handle then get everyone out of the house before calling the fire brigade from a neighbour's house.

If the first warning is a smoke alarm sounding in the middle of the night – or you just smell smoke – then feel the door handle; if it is hot then the fire is probably burning on the other side. You must not open the door; if you do you could be engulfed by flames. Use blankets to block up the underside of the door before going to the window and calling for help.

If the room becomes filled with smoke, put your face as low to the ground as possible – here there will be a few inches of smoke-free air.

In a fire the primary consideration is the lives of people in the house. Never take chances when confronted with a fire or waste precious time gathering possessions.

1

2

3

1 Two sizes of domestic fire extinguisher containing halon; 2 A fire blanket pulls out of a wall-mounted containr; 3 Smoke alarms sound the first alert.

LADDERS AND STEPS

Most do-it-yourselfers find that they need to tackle all sorts of jobs at a variety of heights. Whether the job is simply changing a light bulb or something more adventurous such as mending gutters, it is vital that it should be carried out comfortably and safely. Although everyone readily appreciates the dangers of working on a roof it is not always understood that a fall of just a couple of feet can result in injury. It is essential to have the right equipment for off-the-ground work.

Accident figures prove that using a chair or a shaky stool to stand on to reach a shelf is courting disaster.

For quick, simple jobs such as hanging a picture use a lightweight stepstool. These can be either of timber or aluminium and are available in various heights; some incorporate a grab rail.

When papering a ceiling, you will need to arrange a working platform consisting of strong boards supported at each end on either steps, packing cases, or trestles. On staircases you have to construct a safe arrangement of steps, ladders and boards.

Stepladders or a short ladder will enable you to reach those medium-height jobs. It is worth considering a stepladder which incorporates a shelf at the top on which tools and materials can be stored.

When buying a ladder bear in mind the height of the ladder and the material of which it is constructed.

Most people will want a double extension ladder which will enable them to reach the house gutters in comfort. Remember that you should allow for at least three rungs to extend above the gutters so that, even when working at maximum height, there will still be something to hold on to. Also, remember that a 3m (10ft) double extension ladder will not open up to be 6m (20ft) long. There always has to be an allowance for an overlap of three to four rungs when the ladder is fully extended. This means that a 10ft ladder is likely to be extendable to no more than 5.5m (18ft).

The next factor is whether or not you feel comfortable handling a ladder. Apart from being fairly heavy, all ladders are cumbersome, and awkward things for the inexperienced to handle.

The choice of material lies between timber and aluminium or a mixture of the two. Aluminium ladders are lighter but many people prefer the heavier timber types because they feel more solid although they are in fact exactly the same as aluminium when it comes to safety.

D-shaped rungs are a feature of aluminium ladders and are certainly more comfortable to stand on than are round rungs. If you like you can choose a timber ladder which has aluminium rungs.

Another feature worth inspecting is the feet of a ladder. Good points to look for are such things as rubber end plugs and adjustable feet which can cope with awkward-shaped ground.

Multi-purpose ladders

They come in both wood and aluminium versions. A basic type has a simple hinge/locking mechanism

Bridge windows with a stout batten or a ladder stay. Tie the top to a vine eye in the fascia board.

Stand the ladder on firm, level ground. Prevent slipping by tying or by placing a heavy object against the feet.

which enables it to be converted from a stepladder to a ladder in seconds. A more sophisticated type offers the choice of triple extension ladder, stepladders or, when separated, a single ladder and a pair of steps.

Ladder accessories

Ladder stay Fitted to the top of the ladder to hold it away from the wall. This provides a better working position for painting overhanging eaves or windows or walls.

Tool tray There are many types available which allow you to keep equipment at the top of the ladder. An S-hook is a simple way of supporting a can of paint from a rung.

Roofwork You should never venture on to the roof without the proper equipment. A proper roof ladder has a U-shaped section at the top. The ladder is fixed by running it up the roof (it has rubber-tyred wheels to prevent damage) then turning it over so that the U-section grips the other side of the roof behind the ridge.

Some roof ladders have grab rails fitted, others can accept extension

1 Carry ladder upright so it is well balanced.

2 Fit a ladder stay if needed, when painting eaves, for instance.

3 Raise ladder against the wall; extend if necessary.

4 Pull foot of ladder out from the wall to the correct angle.

pieces where the roof is longer than normal. Also available is a detachable U-shape section which can be fitted to a normal ladder to convert it into a roof ladder.

Loft ladder

Loft ladders fold up into the loft when not in use. There are various makes and none are difficult to fit though in some cases the hatchway might need to be altered slightly.

Safety

Always carry a ladder vertically with one hand holding a low rung and the other holding a rung just above shoulder height to balance it. Resting it against your shoulder makes it more difficult to balance.

A ladder must stand on firm, level ground and lean against something solid. If you are working from a concrete path, rest a sandbag or something similar against the foot to stop the ladder sliding or get someone to support the ladder at the base.

A ladder must never stand on earth – it could sink in or slide fairly easily. Make up a wood platform and nail a length of wood to it – this prevents the ladder slipping. To prevent the platform itself from slipping, drive a couple of strong pegs behind it into the ground.

Using a ladder

If at any time a ladder becomes too heavy to handle, get help.

To raise a ladder, lay it on the ground at right angles to the wall. Then pick up the top rung and walk towards the wall, passing your hands over the rungs as the ladder goes up. When the ladder is against the wall, pull out the foot until the distance between the foot of the ladder and the wall is about a quarter the height of the ladder.

If the ladder has to be extended then do it before pulling the foot out from the wall. Ensure that the overlap between the two sections is ample and that the retaining clips are firmly locked to anchor the top section in place.

When painting on a ladder, right-handed people should work from right to left; the opposite is the case for left-handed people. By doing this, you will always be moving the ladder away from freshly painted work.

Anchor the ladder firmly at the top. Never rest it against a plastic gutter or glass. Only solid walls or boards should be used. If you have to rest the ladder in front of a window, tie the top of the stiles to a 3 × 1in (75 × 25mm) batten which is long enough to rest against the window frame or the wall on either side.

Always tie the top of the ladder to something solid – a window frame makes a good anchorage point. An alternative is to screw a ring bolt to the fascia board or house wall and rope the ladder to it.

Always wear strong shoes (not boots) on a ladder. Standing on trainers will soon cause aching feet.

When you climb a ladder, hold on to the rungs, not the stiles, since this makes the ladder better balanced. Carry tools and equipment in overall pockets or wear a special tool-carrying belt. Alternatively, haul equipment up by rope once you reach the top.

Never go higher than the third rung from the top or you will have nothing to hold on to. Do not stretch too far out to reach a work area – this is dangerous and tiring. Only work within comfortable reach and move the ladder to new areas when necessary.

An arrangement of ladder, steps and scaffold board for decorating stairwell walls and ceiling. Two planks are needed for longer spans

A continuous platform is needed when papering a ceiling

A dual-purpose adjustable ladder used with a scaffold board on stairs. Note: the ladder must be tied to the stairs

Tie and nail boards and pad ladder head for this arrangement on an L-shaped landing and stairs.

SCAFFOLD TOWERS

A scaffold tower is far safer than a ladder because it is more stable; and it provides access to a larger working area. There is plenty of floor space too on a scaffold tower, so you can have all the tools and materials you need at hand, bringing high-level tasks like gutter repairs down to earth. It can be used inside or outside and is great if you have no head for heights and are terrified by ladders.

Surprisingly simple to erect, a 5m (16ft) tower should take two people only a few minutes to build.

Scaffold towers are usually made of aluminium tube and supplied in easy-to-handle H-sections.

The sections are designed to socket into each other but at least one manufacture works with easy-to-climb ladder sections and diagonal braces. Height is increased by adding more ladders and braces.

A sturdy timber platform fits into the top framework. Some towers have platform sections included, while others are offered as optional extras.

Before you buy, study the literature and relate it to the maximum height you wish to reach on your home. In domestic situations bear in mind that if a tower exceeds 3.7m (12ft) you should anchor it to the house to add stability and prevent it from moving. If the tower is to exceed 9.8m (32ft) it must be tied securely into the building at 2.4m (8ft) intervals so that there is no chance of it moving.

A straight-rise tower will have feet to spread the load, and the option of castors to make moving easy. Castors are usable only where the ground is perfectly flat.

For extra stability most companies offer outriggers which, in effect, widen the base.

When used on stairs, sections can be assembled to take in the fall of the stairs and still provide a level working platform.

While a standard tower is capable of taking you to roof level, it is not designed for chimney work. Access to dormer windows can pose a problem, but most scaffolds can be adapted to sit either on a flat roof section or on the sloping roof below a dormer. Again, wherever roof tiles or slates are involved, special feet are available which rest on sandbags laid on the roof. Even on a flat roof section it is wise to spread the load with a plank so that not too much strain is placed upon the roof. If you have this kind of situation, spend time studying the various brochures to see how access is gained.

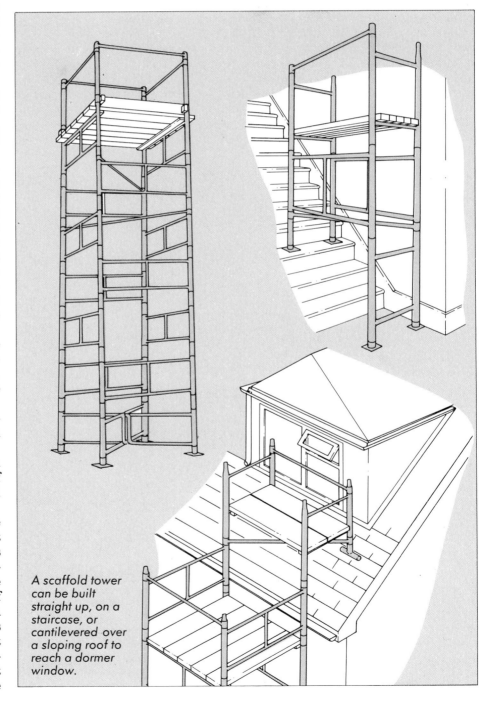

A scaffold tower can be built straight up, on a staircase, or cantilevered over a sloping roof to reach a dormer window.

Apart from the external applications of a tower, there are many uses indoors for at least part of a kit.

Erecting a tower

The first essential is a firm and solid base upon which the tower can stand. The ideal is a concrete path or patio, but if you extend on to a lawn or border, lay down stout timbers upon which the feet of the tower can stand. If you feel there is the slightest chance of movement, tie the frame into the house, however low the tower may be.

Manufacturers supply very clear instructions on how to erect the tower. But do pay attention to details for locking sections together if this is necessary, and for the correct positioning of diagonal braces. Also, before the frame gets too high, check that the tower will be in the correct position to reach the work in hand.

It is vital to check that the frame is going to be vertical. Use a spirit level and the adjustable feet to get the base frames level.

Remember to do all erection work from inside the framework. Climbing up the outside can easily render the tower unstable.

If you need to tie the tower to the house the best way is to use open windows. Place a stout piece of timber horizontally across the window on the inside, then lash rope between this and the frame.

Always climb the inside of the tower and never stand on or climb diagonal braces. Never lean over guard rails. If you cannot reach without stretching, move the tower.

If you use wheels always remember to lock them after moving the tower.

Never move the tower with anyone on board. If you leave tools and materials on the platform make sure that you anchor them so that they cannot roll or slide off.

When you leave the tower standing – perhaps overnight or for a few days – remove the platform. Then make sure that all adjoining windows are shut and securely locked. (You will have to undo temporarily any ropes tied through windows.)

Never let children play on an erected tower.

1 Place foot brace on solid, level ground.

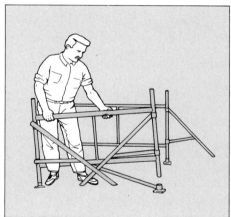

2 Erect the base frame at the foot brace.

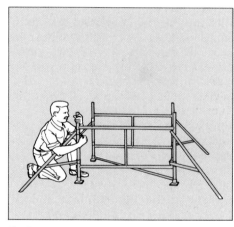

3 Fix outriggers at 45° to the base frames.

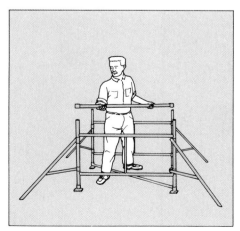

4 Add a cross brace to ensure the frames are square.

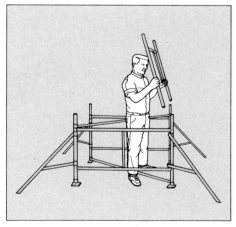

5 Continue to slot in more frames and cross braces.

6 At the top, fix the platform and guard rails.

HOUSEHOLD PESTS

Many pests – insects and rodents – can be prevented from entering the house. Usually they are seeking food and warmth and will be attracted by dirty and unhygienic conditions.

Make a regular check on cupboards. In the loft look out for dead birds or nests in the eaves. Make sure food wastes are disposed of quickly. Check around the house for gaps through which rodents can enter – mice can get through amazingly small holes around waste pipes.

Should you have to kill off an invasion, you will find an arsenal of powders, aerosols and baits available. If an attack gets out of hand, contact your local authority or specialist pest control company.

Ants Worker ants come into the house searching for sweet foods to carry back to the nest and feed the queen. If you can trace the line of ants back to the nest then a kettle of boiling water poured into it will cure the problem. The alternative is to put down a liquid or jelly bait for the ants to take back to the nest and poison the queen. If you do this, expect the number of ants to multiply at first before they die off.

Biscuit beetle Found in food cupboards feeding on crumbs. They can even chew their way into containers. The contents of opened packets of biscuits, cereals, and so on are best kept in airtight plastic containers. The beetles are reddish brown and about 3mm (⅛in) long. They can lurk in crevices, so clean out cupboards thoroughly and puff on an insect powder or spray an aerosol insecticide.

Carpet beetle The larvae are small and hairy and so are also known as woolly bears. They can wander into airing cupboards where they can feed on wool, fabrics and fluff. From here they can be distributed all round the house on sheets, pillowcases and clothes. The beetle is oval shaped, around 3mm (⅛in) long and is a mottled brown and cream colour. Small holes along seams usually indicate its presence. Keep lofts clean; vacuum shelves, upholstery and carpets regularly. Keep woollens, and so on inside sealed polythene bags.

If you spot affected items, spray with a special carpet beetle killer. Puff insecticide powder into crevices or anywhere fluff may collect.

Cockroaches You can tell them from black beetles because of their long antennae and jerky, quick movement. They can be up to 25mm (1in) long. However, you are unlikely to see one since they tend to emerge from their hiding places only at night. They can contaminate food, surfaces and utensils and can cause serious food poisoning. You will have to call in a specialist company if spraying a liberal amount of long-lasting insecticide into likely hiding places fails to do the trick.

Flies They cause food poisoning by contaminating food, so keep all food on surfaces well covered. A flyscreen over an open window is useful. Any flies that do come in can be killed with an aerosol containing pyrethrin. Alternatively, hang up an impregnated strip (not over a food storage area). Dispose of all food waste quickly in sealed bags and keep the dustbin away from open windows or doors.

Earwigs Harmless – just a nuisance. They tend to be brought into the house on cut flowers or they crawl in from wall-climbing plants around windows and doors. Cut back plants around windows and doors and dust corners, windowsills and doorsteps with a dusting powder.

Mice Two types of mouse may be found in the house: the common grey house mouse and the field mouse, which is brown with a white underside and has a long tail and ears. Mice transmit diseases and food poisoning.

The problem is that once inside they can build nests and multiply at a tremendous rate. The telltale signs of a visit are chewed materials and packaging (even cables and water pipes) plus dark coloured droppings. Take remedial action immediately.

Buy some sachets of rodenticide and place one where the mice are known to run – this can be difficult to establish since they are unpredictable. Eventually the attack will cease. The odd mouse can be caught in a traditional mousetrap baited with chocolate or raisins. If you cannot solve the problem quickly, get professional help.

Stop them from getting in again by sealing all likely entry points –

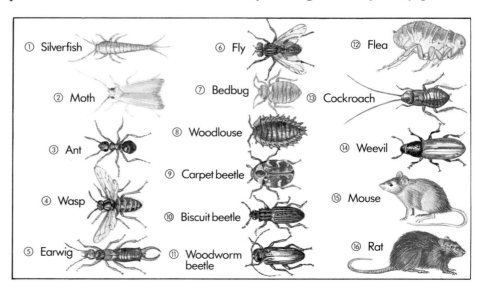

① Silverfish ② Moth ③ Ant ④ Wasp ⑤ Earwig ⑥ Fly ⑦ Bedbug ⑧ Woodlouse ⑨ Carpet beetle ⑩ Biscuit beetle ⑪ Woodworm beetle ⑫ Flea ⑬ Cockroach ⑭ Weevil ⑮ Mouse ⑯ Rat

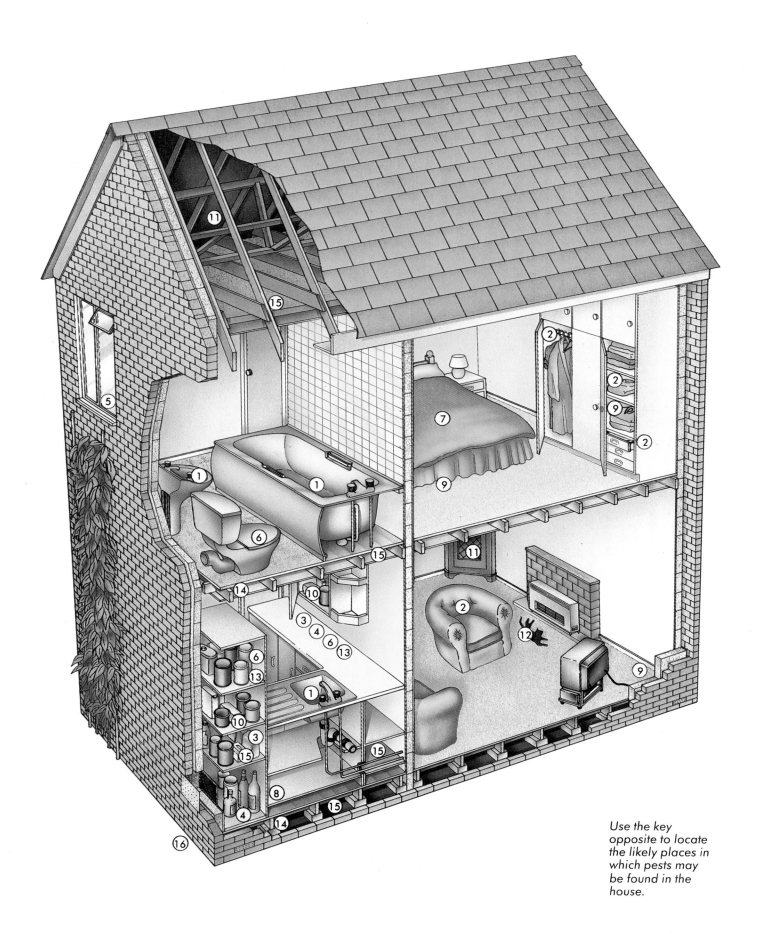

Use the key opposite to locate the likely places in which pests may be found in the house.

Rodents can cause serious damage to electrical installations by their instinctive need to gnaw.

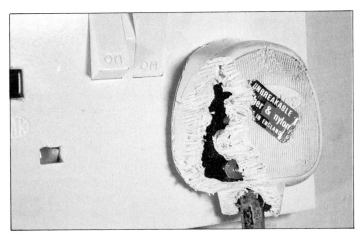

holes in walls and floorboards, gaps below skirtings and so on.

Rats These are filthy creatures that can spread serious diseases and cause food poisoning. They also damage pipes and cables with their constant need to nibble. The common type is the brown rat, which is usually about 225mm (9in) long and has small ears and a tail shorter than the length of its body. It can be brown or almost black in colour. Normally the other type, the black rat, is found only in seaport towns. This has long ears and a tail longer than its body.

In addition to blocking off entry points to the house, you should avoid leaving out bread on the lawn or patio for birds – put it high up on a bird table or hanging basket – otherwise rats will be encouraged to come near the house.

Rats are usually easier to deal with than mice since they tend to stick close to fences and skirtings, following the same path. Place a bait sachet on a known run, allowing the rats to eat it gradually, which might take a day or two. When it has gone, add another sachet until 'visits' cease. It goes without saying that you need expert help with a persistent or major invasion.

Moths The more familiar type has pale, golden wings. This ·is the brown house moth. The other type, the white shouldered house moth, has mottled wings and white head and shoulders. The grubs eat holes in jumpers, carpets, and so on. Man-

made fibres have reduced the moth problem in recent years. Make sure you keep woollen garments clean – moths attack garments having perspiration or urine stains. Store cleaned woollens in sealed polythene bags – and, for good measure, include a moth repellent in the bag. Hang moth repellents in wardrobes. Vacuum-clean carpets regularly and clean out drawers and shelves. If signs of attack are spotted, spray on an aerosol mothproofer paying special attention to seams or folds.

Silverfish These are about 12mm (½in) long and are silvery-grey. They inhabit baths, sinks and bread bins. They eat starchy substances and carbohydrate food deposits. Though harmless in themselves, silverfish do indicate the presence of damp in the house, so the safest cure is to remedy the damp.

Spiders They are harmless – apart from frightening some people. They are also of considerable benefit in catching insect pests. Cobwebs can simply be removed with a brush.

Wasps A summer nuisance, rising to a peak in August. They will sting if threatened. A fly screen across an open window prevents entry and an insecticidal aerosol will kill an intruder searching for sweetstuffs.

If you find a wasp nest in the garden, treat it at dusk when all the wasps have returned for the night. Wear gloves and puff wasp nest killer into the entrance. Allow a couple of days then, with hands and face protected, dig out the nest, spraying

with insecticide at the same time.

Woodlice These are about 12mm (½in) long, with oval, grey, segmented bodies. They may curl up when disturbed. Normally they live in the garden under stones and plants but if they do enter the house they will live under a doormat or in dark, cool corners.

They do not usually stay inside very long but if they persist, then check and remedy the cause of any dampness. Get rid of any rotting wood, on which they like to feed. Puff or spray long-lasting insecticides around door thresholds or other likely entry points.

Woodworm There are several types of wood beetle, the most common being the furniture beetle, but all are generally called woodworm. The larva of the beetle chews its way through wood, creating little tunnels, for a couple of years until it breaks back on to the surface where it turns into an adult (leaving behind the familiar hole in the surface). The adults then mate, the female lays more eggs in the wood, the larvae hatch and start to tunnel into the wood. And so the cycle continues. If left unchecked woodworm can cause serious structural damage, although the speed at which this will happen depends on the species and location.

Structural timbers in lofts, floor joists, floorboards and staircases are at risk – any untreated wood is especially vulnerable. You can treat the woodworm yourself by spraying or brushing on a good woodworm killer. The job must be done thoroughly, which means cleaning surfaces scrupulously, taking up floorboards as necessary so that all parts of the wood are treated.

Pay attention to the manufacturer's instructions and wear protective clothing while doing the job. Spray all the timbers in the area – not just those obviously attacked.

Furniture can be treated using cans of woodworm fluid with a special injector nozzle to force the fluid into the holes. A woodworm killing polish, applied occasionally, will resist future attacks.

INDEX